Sustain The Flame

- reflections on this MLA's foray into Facebook and Twitter.

Barry McElduff

In memory of Aoife,
loving Mother of Oisin;
Mrs. Annie Kelly, Paula's Mother;
and all my deceased relatives on the
McElduff and McGurk sides of our family
(nach maireann agus atá ar shlí na fírínne anois).

Contents

Buíochas / Acknowledgement

I want to express my gratitude and appreciation to Nova Print in West Belfast for helping me to deliver this, my second book. Aidan and Denis are more than printers. They are good craic, creative and professional to the last.

As ever, I owe a lot to many of my Sinn Féin colleagues who helped me specifically in relation to writing SUSTAIN THE FLAME; Helena McElhone, Catherine Kelly, Barry McColgan, Raymond McNally, Brian Quinn, Des Donnelly and Phil Flanagan.

Also, my cousin, Malachy McGuone from Creggan but who currently lives in London; and Carrickmore Youth Club Senior Members' Committee.

They each gave me valuable feedback on what I was setting out to achieve with this publication.

In addition, I want to express my thanks to Oliver Corr Photography. I also wish to record my appreciation to the all-female team at RUA in Pomeroy. It was Donna and Niamh, in particular, who offered me wise counsel on how to develop a social media strategy in the first instance.

When it comes to inspirational bloggers, by the way, I would put Jude Collins top of the list. Of course, Jude is 'originally' from Omagh and that helps to some degree at least.

Jude is courageous, honest and thought-provoking. This section seems as appropriate as any other for saluting him and his blogs. Quality man.

Oh, and did I thank my family yet? No.
Ba mhaith liom mo bhuíochas a ghabháil le Paula, Niamh, Bláthnaid agus Patrick. KHL or should I say, STF !

And finally, my loyal followers who are always quick off the mark to 'like', 'comment' or 'share' my musings on Facebook and Twitter.

Everyone needs positivity and encouragement in their worlds.

Introduction

I simply need to get it out there: I am in my fiftieth year. There, that is sorted now and out in the open. I can now proceed.

2016 is a big year all round, then, both for those of us who were born in 1966, reaching our 50th le cuidiú Dé, and for those of us who are proud to celebrate the Easter Rising of 1916 in its centenary year.

SUSTAIN THE FLAME sounds more sophisticated than its rural cousin, KEEP 'ER LIT, a slightly more up-market variation of a title for my second book. **STF** is partly a wee update of sorts on my early KHL memoirs which I wrote three years ago.

I succeeded in reaching my target audience then and this brought me a considerable amount of craic and personal satisfaction in the process.

But you know me. I couldn't leave it at that. I have more to say.

When my teenage son, Patrick heard that I was writing another book, he was probably mindful of the potential embarrassment factor for him within his peer group when he cautioned me to 'wise up' and told me:

"Please, Daddy. You are NOT Harry Potter!"

When you reach 'my age', nearly the big fifty, remember, a little reflection is required.

This book is really an exercise in reflection on the past year or so.

It was during this period that I took the conscious decision to embrace social media: Facebook, Twitter and my very own weekly blog.

I am not 'a natural' so to speak when it comes to technology but I knew that I simply had to embrace social media. Standing still in this world doesn't seem to work.

Either that or be left behind in a world where you have to re-invent yourself every now and then to keep up.

It would appear that if you have a message to convey, a cause to promote and if you wish to remain current and relevant to younger people, then you simply cannot afford to ignore *Facebook* or *Twitter*.

I still love leafing through newspapers in my hand even if they get out of shape and it takes some folding and re-arranging to sort them out, especially broadsheets.

The hard copies of The Ulster Herald, An Phoblacht, The Irish News and The Irish Times still matter to me.

I prefer, in fact, to read a paper the conventional way.
But the world has changed and many do all or most of their reading online.

How many 'friends', 'likes', 'shares', 'followers', 'favourites' and 'retweets' you have is the currency of today for many trying to gauge the effectiveness of their communications strategy.

The first practical thing that I did then was to upgrade from a Blackberry to an I Phone before I was ready to boogie.

The second initiative that I took was to drive six miles to take some sensible advice from Donna, Niamh and the RUA Digital team based at The Rowan Centre in Pomeroy.

I certainly benefitted from wise counsel from young minds. **'SUSTAIN THE FLAME'** is a reflection on my *tyronemansblog* and on my *Facebook* posts and *tweets* in the past year.

I do this not for the sake of it but to analyse the content of 'my digital footprint' and to tell my story, through the prism of social media and my year in relation to politics, the GAA and community.

What else would this former corner forward for Carrickmore and current Omagh- based Sinn Féin MLA write about ?

Twitter is the platform which most attracts abusive, personalised comments, I think. Very often the twitter account of the abuser is anonymous or hiding behind a pseudonym.

This might explain why I prefer the platform of Facebook where more real people inhabit the space and where the comments are mostly constructive and engaging.

This book is more focussed on the medium of Facebook and on my blog than it is on my twitter output.

For the uninitiated, I describe my blog as a weekly essay, as if back at school, which is available to read every Friday around midday.

Now let us take a look together at what connected and what counted most during my initial foray into the world of social media.

Vox audita perit litera scripta manet
A heard voice perishes, but the written letter remains.

November 2015

Facebook

www.facebook.com/barrymcelduff

*'Better to write for yourself
and have no public, than to write for the public
and have no self.'*
Cyril Connolly
(The New Statesman, February 25, 1933).

You never know when you might need a man in Beijing

Barry Mc Elduff
Big Joe from Tattyreagh is busy booking accommodation for the trip to Tipp. Joe is for the match in Thurles and possibly the Fleadh in Nenagh as well if he can do the two. Tír Eoin Abú !

Barry Mc Elduff's photos in Mobile Uploads · 17 July ·
View Full Size · Send as message · Report Photo

Joe Gallagher scored 184 points out of 200 in his Mandarin Chinese exam at Omagh College.
When I wrote this in my mid-September blog, people who know Joe shared it with each other.

One sent it on to Joe's nephew, Mícheál with the comment that Joe 'is once again setting the bar high for you boys.'

Another reckoned that Joe's new language skills 'would come in very useful around Tattyreagh'.

Joe shared his achievement privately with me and I decided to share it with the wider world without seeking or receiving his express approval.

He just laughed when one of his friends rang him from Glasgow to congratulate him. I asked Joe why he undertook to learn Chinese and he winked at me and said, "intelligence wins the war and before this is over, we might need men in Beijing."

It was earlier in the summer that I posted a photo of Joe, sitting in the passenger seat of my car at the rear of our offices at James Street in Omagh with a mobile phone to his ear.

Joe was heading to Thurles to support Tyrone in the 'Back Door' Qualifiers that weekend but he had a notion of attending the Fleadh in Nenagh when he was down that length.

He was phoning to check on the availability of a room anywhere in Tipperary because he had left it a bit late.

Joe is a mighty man for the road. Sometimes he sends me a text from the Galway Races wondering if I am about.

Joe thinks that everybody should be there or should at least put the Galway Races in their diary for next year

I give Michael 10 out of 10 every day

Barry Mc Elduff
Michael Murphy laid the ball off to this corner forward earlier today and he went for the return pass.

Barry Mc Elduff's photos in Mobile Uploads · 23 July ·
View Full Size · Send as message · Report Photo

I just happened to meet five Donegal GAA supporters in the KFC in Armagh three hours after Mayo beat them in this year's All Ireland Quarter Final.

I knew Marie Therese Gallagher (Comhairleoir), 'one of our own' from Gaoth Dobhair, within the group but I did not know the other four who were with her.

It was probably a stupid question but I asked each of them to name their favourite Donegal player 'of all time'.

None of the five showed the slightest hesitation before one name, and one name only, featured in the five separate responses.

That name was Michael Murphy.

I am proud to say I know Michael personally. In fact, I know several Michael Murphys.

In truth I hugely admire two of them: one, the main man himself from Glenswilly and the other, the life-long Republican from Rostrevor, usually referred to as Mick.

I have met Michael on a number of occasions and I pinch myself like a chid when he remembers my name.

I am never shy of standing up for myself or my beliefs when the occasion demands but I tend to be a wee bit in awe of certain Gaelic football legends. It is just the way I am.

That is why I respected so much the concentration levels, the determination and at times 'unpleasantness' of Justin McMahon when he carried off the tightest ever man-marking job on Michael Murphy in the Ulster Championship first round match played in Ballybofey in May of this year.

Any man who can 'legally' prevent Michael Murphy from playing football for seventy minutes is himself worthy of top marks.

I have never witnessed anything like it in my life, the way that Justin McMahon stuck to Michael Murphy that day.

And I give Michael top marks every day.

Sometimes Celine accompanies me up the M1

Barry Mc Elduff

Was listening to high powered Celine Dion songs which made references to the wind and elements and to driving through the night as I returned home in the early hours of the morning after yesterday's lengthy sitting of the Assembly. The M1 and the various country roads were full of leaves and debris at that hour.

Back in Stormont today for another lengthy sitting, this time focusing in the evening on the Education Bill.

I cannot imagine that Oscar and Cahir will have made it to school today following yesterday's marathon session.

Barry Mc Elduff's photos in Timeline Photos · 21 October 2014 · View Full Size · Send as message · Report Photo

 Like   💬 Comment   ➤ Share

People usually access their music online nowadays, too, but me, I'm still a CD man. Before that, it was tapes, and before tapes there were records, including LPs.

I have a good wee collection of CDs in my 2007 Toyota Auris. They assume great importance when I am commuting back and forward to Stormont.

This is especially so after a late night sitting On The Hill and I am driving back down the M1, sometimes well after midnight when a diversion sign for roadworks at Junction 12 is the last thing in the world that you want to see.

It can be cold and windy for sure on the M1 late at night and the wind can shake your wee car from time to time as well.

My choice of musical accompaniment varies depending on the mood and depending on the proximity of a particular CD.

I have put up posts to record that I have listened to Celine Dion, to Whitney, to Donna Taggart from Clanabogan to Luther Vandross or to Simply Red.

I have received some negative feedback about listening to Mick Hucknall but never any negative regarding the other four.

And anyway, it is my musical choice and I do have 'editorial' control over this decision at least.

'Dance with my father' is the classic father / son song, as far as I am concerned, and sometimes I play it over and over again.

It defines Luther Vandross for me.

Is it illegal to be patriotic in Ireland?

Barry Mc Elduff
We remember IRA Volunteers today from all generations and all phases of struggle. Fuair siad bás ar son saoirse na hÉireann.

Barry Mc Elduff's photos in Mobile Uploads · 5 April ·
View Full Size · Send as message · Report Photo

This Easter Sunday past, I had speaking duties in both Drumragh and Carrickmore. The following day took me to Enniscorthy where I addressed Republicans from different parts of Wexford. They gathered to do the very same thing as we had done in Tyrone the previous day.

That was to honour and remember Ireland's patriot dead.

When I think of Loch Garman, I think of purple and gold and of the hurling men of '96, including my friend, Dave Guiney. I think of Vinegar Hill and who fears to speak of '98.

On my way to speak at the grave of another good friend and deceased Sinn Féin activist, Colm Grimes on the Sunday, I pulled in outside McDonald's on the Dromore Road, Omagh because there is always WiFi in or near McDonald's the world over.

I wanted to put up a post which was simple and to the point. This way I could reach more people than the number who would show up in person in Drumragh.

I included a poster image of the Volunteers killed by the British Army at Loughgall in County Armagh, among them Paula's beloved brother, Patrick Kelly from Dungannon.

'It appears to me that Ireland is one of the few countries in the world where it is illegal to be patriotic,' a former pupil of Drumragh Integrated College from Omagh said to me when he came to me for work experience.

Matthew put it very well.

The IRA called a cessation of its military operations over twenty years ago. They did this as a proud, undefeated army which had strong community support the length and breadth of Ireland as well as abroad. Any of them I ever knew were decent, politically motivated people who had so much to live for.

To assert such a truth on Facebook and more especially on Twitter nowadays would be certain to provoke a nasty response from trolls, keyboard warriors and The News Letter.

Every one of us, from Aghyaran to Ardboe

RTÉ apologise to MLA over 'Tyrone tweet confusion'

John Monaghan

RTÉ has apologised for "any confusion" after appearing to endorse a tweet which expressed hope that Kerry "knock seven shades out of these Tyrone lads" ahead of the All-Ireland semi-final.

Sinn Féin West Tyrone MLA Barry McElduff (pictured) complained about the tweet which was posted by former Meath footballer Anthony Moyles and 'favourited' by the Sunday Game account.

At the time Mr McElduff said he had made the complaint as it "almost confirms that there is a feeling of anti-Tyrone bias inside RTÉ."

Moyles said he hoped "Kerry knock seven shades out of these Tyrone lads ...that (Tiernan) McCann lad needs a serious lesson given to him," a reference to the defender who collapsed to the turf in the quarter final after Monaghan's Darren Hughes ruffled his hair.

In response to the complaint RTÉ said the 'favouriting' of comments is "merely for referencing purposes."

A Sunday Game spokesman said: "It is in effect a bookmarking service that allows us to tag certain comments that we may wish to come back to for future reference purposes.

"In no way would we ever insinuate that using the favourite option would be in any way an endorsement of those views."

The spokesman added: "We apologise for any confusion this may have caused as it wasn't our intention for it to be perceived in such a fashion."

Mr McElduff told *The Irish News* he "welcomed that RTÉ have addressed the issue."

He said: "It is not appropriate for RTÉ to favourite a tweet of this nature. It might be a bit creative of RTÉ to suggest that this is merely a bookmarking exercise."

The Sinn Féin MLA added: "Moyles is partisan and is entitled to be so. However RTÉ lowered their standard in 2015 and I would like them to raise their game for 2016, as Tyrone intend to do also."

I dialled the number for RTÉ and asked to speak to Noel Curran, Director General of our national broadcaster.

Noel wasn't in the office at the time but his PA, Lynn Davis undertook to pass my message to him. Yes, and the obligatory *'Can you put your complaint in an e-mail and send it to me ?'*

And so I did, seeking an explanation as to why the flagship 'Sunday Game' had favourited a tweet from former Meath player, Anthony Moyles which revealed more than a little bias against the Tyrone football team.

In our world, that means every single one of us in Tyrone, from Aghyaran to Ardboe and everywhere in between.

There has been a troubled relationship between RTÉ and Tyrone this past number of years and Uachtarán himself, Áogan Ó Fearghail has said that he finds RTÉ's criticism of Tyrone and other Ulster counties to be 'negative', 'fairly predictable' and 'tiresome.'

Pat Fahy attributes this to the scourge of partitionism, plain and simple, within the southern establishment, including RTÉ.

Anyway, I was promised a response from David McKenna, Head of Complaints within twenty working days, with the deadline set for Friday 11 September.

Fix the bleedin' clock and be done with it!

Barry Mc Elduff

As well as needing to achieve neutrality with symbols and emblems over Omagh Courthouse, they need to fix the bleedin' clock.

You would be surprised at the number of people in Omagh who have mentioned to me the fact that the clock above the Courthouse is never on the right time.

I contacted the Courts Service during the week and initially they were unaware that the clock was wrong. Then their PR strategy kicked in and they talked about needing a specialist to come from England and as well as 'financial constraints'. Good one !

I reckon that there has to be someone in the Omagh area or wider County Tyrone who could fix this clock in a cost effective manner.

I attracted some support but also some unexpected and unfavourable 'digs' and jibes about a post which I put up on 13 November 2014 concerning the town clock in Omagh.

This clock, on the top of Omagh Courthouse is never on the right time; never ever.

'Had I nothing better to be doing with my time and could I not get Roads Service to fill in a few potholes?'

Yes, I am fully aware that there are bigger problems in the world. We still face partition, occupation, poverty, injustice and war on an unacceptable scale and we all have to do our bit to combat climate change as well.

In the overall scheme of things, the town clock in Omagh might not seem too important but it did catch my eye when I stopped outside the Postal Sorting Office in High Street to check the time.

Apparently 'everybody' has an iPhone nowadays and 'nobody' wears a watch or looks at the Town Clock.

The Blame Game comedians had a go at me about this in The Strule Arts Centre and on the televised version of the show, too.

It was meat and drink to Jake O'Kane and Colm Murphy who said that the Shinners would know all about timers alright.

If a town clock was togging out to contest a county final, it would want to be on the right time.

SUSTAIN THE FLAME
Some would nearly tweet from the Requiem Mass

I cannot change

Courage to

change the things I can

and the Wisdom

to know the difference

Barry Mc Elduff
Throughout the week, I have been involved in wee battles and 'scrapes' with individuals and various organisations, mostly on behalf of other people but some on my own behalf. I have attended football matches where, at the time, the outcome of the match made it seem as if it was the end of the world.
However, I have also spoken this week to people who have major health worries at this time and I am very conscious of tragedies happening around us, both locally and further afield which help to put things into perspective for me and for all of us.
Serenity would be a great thing.

Barry Mc Elduff's photos in Timeline Photos · 15 October 2014 ·
View Full Size · Send as message · Report Photo

I tend not to touch the subject of death in my blog or on Facebook.

For me, not always, but most of the time, it just doesn't feel entirely appropriate.

These forms of media are too new, too untried, too untrustworthy for the solemnity of the moment.

There is no facility for not being sure of whether to speak or not.

There are those who would nearly tweet from the Requiem Mass. I am not one of them.

If I am asked by the media to comment on the death of someone, I always feel more sure of my footing and of my territory if I have already shaken the hand of the bereaved family members in private.

If I haven't sympathised in person, I make that very point, that it might be better to wait.

The reason that I speak at all in these circumstances is because sometimes, in the case of a particular tragedy, for example, or in the case of a prominent local person dying, it might fall to me as a public representative to extend sympathy 'on behalf of the wider community.'

It can be important, too, to convey to the family that they are 'highly respected' in the local community. People sometimes don't appreciate that simple truth until it is actually said out loud by someone about them.

On one occasion, I merely posted The Serenity Prayer as a response to the suddenness of the death of a young person whose parents are known to me.

An elected representative such as an MLA or a TD doesn't always know for sure what is the correct thing to say or do, either.

I wouldn't rule out absolutely using Facebook to communicate sympathy but so far, it just hasn't felt right or proper for me to do so.

Try telling that to the people of

Barry Mc Elduff
Real good engagement at last night's meeting in Eskra about broadband and mobile phone coverage. A lot of info to absorb and a lot to reflect on. Fair play to BT, O2 and Vodafone for coming into the lion's den...I will reflect with others on how to take rural equality campaign to next level.
Many thanks to MCK TechPro Events, a local company who helped us out with sound and mics. Very professional.

Barry Mc Elduff's photos in Timeline Photos · 6 February ·

One issue which comes up most days and definitely several times a week at least: Broadband.

As an MLA, I campaign relentlessly for better broadband coverage in rural parts of West Tyrone.

Mostly that means making contact with senior people in BT. At least I have good access and it is much better than the customer trying to communicate with a call centre thousands of miles away.

During the past year, Glenn Campbell, Stephen McCann, Barry McNally (Councillors) and I also organised a rather grandly named Rural Telecommunications Summit in Eskra. This was very well attended because we effectively brought the mountain to Mohammed.

Literally anybody who was anybody from the world of broadband and the mobile phone industry was at the top table.

Such was the level of engagement from the floor of the meeting and informally on the margins of the meeting that those officials and company reps could have benefitted from a stiff drink in The Bridge Tavern afterwards.

More recently in August, I had a meeting with Minister Jonathan Bell who has some responsibility for Telecommunications. His Department likes to boast of 100% coverage 'in the region' but try telling that to people in Eskra or Creggan 'til you see how you get on.

No words of explanation were necessary

Barry Mc Elduff
Vincent McAnespie and Mickey Muldoon raising the
Slaughtneil flag at the spot where Aidan, Vincent's
brother was murdered by the British Army on
Aughnacloy border.

Barry Mc Elduff's photos in Mobile Uploads · 17 March ·

I had to turn the car around and go back to Aidan
McAnespie's monument. It was the morning of the All
Ireland Club Finals in Football and Hurling and I was en
route to Croke Park.

As I approached the grounds of Aghaloo GAC on the outskirts of Aughnacloy, I caught a glimpse of Vincent McAnespie, Aidan's brother, and another man raising the maroon and white flag of Slaughtneil over the roadside monument to my right.

Sure as God, there was Vincent and his good friend, Mickey Muldoon raising the flag.

I got it straightaway. The connection. The poignancy of the moment. And because I understood it, no words were necessary.

The spot where Aidan was shot dead by a British soldier at the permanent checkpoint on his way to an Aghaloo / Killeeshil match in February 1988 is of huge symbolic importance to people far and near.

I asked Vincent and Mickey if they wouldn't mind and they didn't, so I took a picture of the two men duly raising the Slaughtneil flag.

On the very morning when this valiant Gaelic community from South Derry were preparing to take on Corofin of Galway at Headquarters.

I posted the photo and a brief comment and it travelled as a post far further than I could have imagined.

If I had any doubts about the popularity and reach of Aidan's family, these were totally allayed when I used a photo image of young Ryan, Vincent's son when he made his National Football League debut for Monaghan at Healy Park in Omagh.

My blog that week reached its highest ever number, in fact, well in excess of 25,000, I think.

You would hate to fall out with Aidan McAnespie's people and they are relations of my own of course.

Danny told me to "always close the gate"

Barry Mc Elduff
I first canvassed with Danny Morrison over thirty years ago. Danny told me to always close gates after me.

Barry Mc Elduff's photos in Mobile Uploads · 1 May ·

I was surprised at the popularity of the post which showed me closing a gate in Strathroy after I had canvassed a local family ahead of the Westminster elections in early May.

Not closing a gate can get you into trouble. These things matter when you are on the canvass trail.

So does knocking a door when the parents are putting the children to bed or when Coronation Street is on the TV.

Dogs pose a real threat to the canvasser, too, but of course the owner will say, "He wouldn't touch you."

And then they express surprise because 'he never did that before.'

There does be some real engagement on the doorsteps and you do pick up a lot of important constituency messages this way.

One woman said to me that she always voted for Sinn Féin but that she might not on this occasion because she doesn't agree with everything that Sinn Féin does or says.

I advised her to vote for us if she agreed with us on eight out of ten issues but I also told her that I heard an American politician saying that 'if you agree with me on ten out of ten points, see your psychiatrist.'

Either way, you have to close the gate behind you if that is the way you found it when you arrived.

One of the many wisdoms I learned during my political apprenticeship with Danny Morrison thirty years ago.

MLAs deal with real issues all the time

Barry Mc Elduff added **2 new photos**.

27 August at 09:46 · Edited ·

BREAKING: Delighted that the four separate GP Practices in Omagh Health Centre now have local rate phone numbers. These are listed in today's Ulster Herald (Page 10). 0844 Numbers were/are premium rate / high cost. As MLA, I have been lobbied extensively on this.

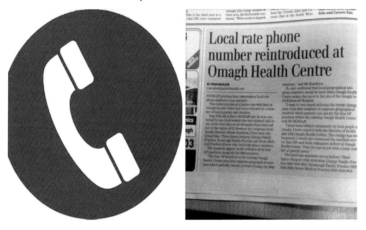

The media like to present 'politicians' as not having anything to say about what they describe as the 'real issues.'

As if we are concerned only with 'flegs' and arguments with our opponents.

But if you were to contact the same media about a 'real issue' they will very often tell you that the programme or the paper is 'already full.'

They have no space left for your 'real' story about current emigration patterns or the latest update in the campaign to secure the A5 Road.

Facebook can be funny (rare), too, because a trivial comment can provoke many responses while something very serious and very substantive might generate next to no response.

I was delighted that Omagh Health Centre re-introduced local rate phone calls after having used a premium rate call system for several years.

I lobbied for this change and there was a successful outcome. When I communicated the end of the high cost call system, it attracted little interest on Facebook.

Must be that younger people do not lift the phone too often to the Health Centre and those who do are a different age demographic and are not on Facebook.

I know I was lobbied extensively about this by older people in the main...thereby explaining the small number of likes and comments online for this bit of good news.

I am convinced they have saved lives

Barry Mc Elduff

Does anyone be on Facebook after 1am ? Probably not too many. Let me pay tribute to Omagh Street Safe Volunteers Ryan, Hazel, Brian and Rosella who are on 'til 3am offering support to anyone in difficulty in town tonight. I dropped by to say thanks earlier.

Barry Mc Elduff's photos in Mobile Uploads · 30 August ·

I had been in Dungannon that morning; Ballinamore, County Leitrim in the afternoon and Trillick in the evening.

I was now on my way home from the hugely successful 'Strictly Red' in Trillick. It was well after midnight and I was tired.

Driving down High Street in Omagh, I sensed that the town was quiet but I still knew that this would soon change, as per every Saturday night when Sally's, Main Street and the other pubs and night-spots would say 'oíche mhaith' to their many patrons. I saw to my left the white gazebo in front of the Public Services Centre where those out for the night could stop off for tea and a chat with local people who volunteer their time to make the streets safer for everyone.

Ryan Tracey was the first Volunteer I met and he was preparing to go out on patrol, you could say, down by the River Bank and the new Oasis area at the Ulsterbus depot.

He and Brian, aided by Rosella and Hazel put together everything they would need by way of first aid kit, water, flip flops (to replace high heels) and whatever else they might need should they come across someone in a state of distress or disorientation.

Ryan and Brian had two-way radios and all the proper gear complete with torch for the job. Rosella and Hazel would continue to staff their post at the gazebo.

I took a photo of the team and posted it on Facebook to show my appreciation for all the Omagh Street Safe Volunteers as their local MLA and it attracted massive interest online as evidenced by the likes and supportive comments.

Many just wanted to say thanks and other Volunteers, including Michelle Cox of Drumragh GAC fame, Monica Coyle from Greencastle and Aidy McHugh from Drumquin wanted to acknowledge this public demonstration of appreciation.

They are fully trained up and they do this work on a voluntary basis in shifts at weekends. They usually stay on 'til 3am or so, I am led to believe when, as Spike Milligan once said, 'everyone else is at home and in their beds.'

I know these people have saved lives. There is plenty of anecdotal evidence to back this up.

Hands off St Mary's, Stephen

Barry Mc Elduff
Only arrived home from Stormont after midnight. Late debate was on the future of St Mary's University College in Belfast.

Alex Maskey allowed me an intervention in the debate to draw attention to the close connection that many families and communities in rural parts of the north, including Donegal and Monaghan have had with St Mary's for over 100 years.

Alliance's Stephen Farry does not like this institution which has a strong Irish identity and which has produced high quality teachers and leaders all down the years.

I say, Hands Off, Farry and KHL, St Mary's.

Tá súil agam go mbeidh an Coláiste beo agus laidir sna blianta atá romhann.

Barry Mc Elduff's photos in Timeline Photos · 28 January ·
View Full Size · Send as message · Report Photo

We debated the future of St. Mary's University College in the Assembly Chamber at Stormont late into the night at the end of January.

The Alliance Party Minister for Employment and Learning seemed to be on an ideological crusade against St. Mary's and was evidently trying to close it down by stealth.

Our Belfast MLAs were to the fore in defending the University College and putting it up to Stephen Farry.

I made the point that St. Mary's was everyone's business, everyone's concern.

In Tyrone, for example, the reputation of St. Mary's is excellent.

I hate it when people try to fix things that are not broken.

Thousands of teachers and leaders in our communities have been trained and educated at St. Mary's down the years.

Yes, it has a Catholic ethos and it promotes Gaelic Games, culture agus an Ghaeilge í féin.

Yes, it is situated on the Falls Road in West Belfast and yes, it acts as an economic driver for a socially disadvantaged community.

Yes, our MP in that community, Paul Maskey was leading the fight along with the students and staff.

I was pleased that Sinn Féin ministers were subsequently able to give the red card to Stephen Farry's proposals at the Executive table.

Wouldn't it be great to see 'The Ranch' prosper long into the future.

Coláiste Ollscoile Naomh Muire Abú.

John does his best despite Tory cuts

Barry Mc Elduff

I delivered more letters from school communities in West Tyrone to Education Minister John O'Dowd at Stormont yesterday afternoon (Wednesday).

John took time to read a sample of these letters there and then and he gave a commitment to take careful note of all the points that we are making about the Draft Education Budget. The letter that he is reading in this picture is from Maura Dolan, Principal of Holy Family P.S in Omagh.

When I lobbied John O'Dowd as Education Minister in the North variously and throughout 2014/2015 about the needs of our local school communities, John always did his best to deliver but often emphasised how the Tory government in London was crippling his efforts.

At local level, school principals and teachers put pressure on me to improve their situation whether that be a new mobile classroom in time for September or the retention of valued staff, including classroom assistants.

This is fiercely frustrating at this time.

Sometimes John and his Department are able to deliver but on other occasions, John, like any other local Minister would tell you that he has simply been denied 'a workable budget' to do the things he would like and need to do to further improve educational outcomes.

John has been right of course but this can be difficult to communicate to local people who are campaigning for proper school accommodation or other support for their school.

I always show John the letters and emails which I receive and I do know for certain that he tries his absolute best in all circumstances.

I personally delivered a sackful of lobbying letters to the Department of Education in Bangor, County Down between Christmas and the New Year.

In truth, those letters could more properly have been diverted to the Tories in Westminster because it is they who are crippling our public services.

Any wonder Sinn Féin refuses to demean itself and our people by becoming agents for delivering Tory cuts in this part of Ireland.

By this stage, the dead sheep had drifted as far as Newtown

Barry Mc Elduff
Was on my way to lunch in Serendipity in Bridge Street, Omagh today, a lunch date with none other than Peter the Great, if you don't mind when my attention was drawn by a number of young people to two dead sheep at the weir on the River Strule, quite close to the Strule Arts Centre and to Omagh College.

Such a shame when the River Strule is so important to visitors and anglers. In fact, the River Strule is one of the best rivers for fishing for salmon in the whole of Ireland.

I have been trying to pin down who is responsible for addressing this situation...is it Omagh District Council Environmental Health Department or is it Loughs Agency.

Also spoke to Tyrone Herald about this. I just want the dead animals removed asap and a renewed approach to prevent this type of thing in the future. Not good.

Barry Mc Elduff's photos in Timeline Photos · 24 October 2014 · View Full Size · Send as message · Report Photo

There is so much happening in this Facebook post. Firstly, you might gather that I had just come across two dead sheep in the River Strule. They were stuck in the weir.

Secondly, I was having lunch with Peter, a fact but also a bit of a throwaway boast from one legendary forward referring to another. Outside the county, this provokes commentary like 'you lot keep it tight in Tyrone.'

Thirdly, our lunch was in 'Serendipity' in Bridge Street (quite difficult to spell but 'class' when you get there). And yes, in response to one of the Fb comments, Stephanie O'Kane did feed us very well.

There is a concern for the environment at the heart of this post but I heard after the event that the two dead sheep had subsequently been dislodged by the current and had reached Newtown by then.

I say 'Newtown' here because the late Tommy McNamee told me never to recognise the Stewarts who dispossessed his people of their land in the first instance.

Anyway, when the sheep crossed over from the Omagh district to the Strabane district and on into the Mourne, it was no longer the responsibility of the Council in Omagh, which meant that I now had to contact Environmental Health in Strabane.

By the way, Peter ordered a BLT Sandwich which I had not heard of previously.

He probably knows all the different types of coffee, too, from Cappuccino to Latté.

'Tis far from Lattés we were all reared.

James McClean's cousin is also a sound man

Barry Mc Elduff

I hear that Martin O'Neill plans to have 'a wee chat' with James McClean, as 'coach to player' about recent happenings. Sound. Perhaps Martin should listen, too, because James appears to me to have something worthwhile to say, as well, you know.

Barry Mc Elduff's photos in Mobile Uploads · 27 July · View Full Size · Send as message · Report Photo

Young people I know look up to James McClean. They like the fact that he is true to his identity and true to his upbringing in the Creggan area of Derry. They like his courage.

I know a relation of James' and he, Paul, is a sound man, too. James is a professional soccer player for West Bromwich Albion in England who also plays for the Irish 'international' team.

I put the inverted commas around the word 'international' in this context because it will only truly qualify for this description when there is an all-Ireland team, incorporating the Six Counties as well.

For his part, James lets it be known that he is a big fan of the music of The Wolfe Tones and that he doesn't particularly want to wear a poppy or stand upright for the English National Anthem.

He has his reasons for this.

James likes being himself but some sections of the media like to present him as a 'controversialist' who is seeking attention.

James is the subject of serious criticism and some soccer fans in England boo loudly every time he touches the ball.

More than anything, I suspect that James would love to do what he does best without any fuss or attention.

BBC Newsreaders and even contestants on ITV's X Factor are compelled to wear the poppy whether they or their families approve or not, as far as I believe.

I am not sure what would be the ultimate sanction for any conscientious objector who declined to read the news when they are forced to wear a poppy while doing so.

You can speak when you have championship medals

Barry Mc Elduff

See below report from Teamtalkmag.com of our great under 16 success yesterday. Once again, Ciaran Daly lifted the shield as captain and he shared the speech making responsibilities at Quinn's Corner with his able vice-captain, Conor Loughran.

This team made history. KHL.

Teamtalkmag.com said:

Carrickmore completed a league and championship under 16 double when they defeated Dromore in the league final on Sunday afternoon.

The winners laid the foundations for victory in a wind assisted first half when they opened up a 2-7 to 0-0 lead with Ciaran Cuddy and Padraig Mc Elduff finding the net for the winners.

Championship medals are much sought after where I come from.

Plunkett 'Big Oz' McCallan is one of only a handful of footballers in Tyrone who are in possession of six Senior Championship medals.

No-one has more than six.

2014 nearly brought Oz his elusive seventh medal against Omagh St. Enda's but he was to be so cruelly denied this by a late winning goal which came from the boot of Ronan O'Neill. Not that Ronan O'Neill cared much for Oz' feelings at the time.

Our Patrick has two Championship medals so far: Under 13 and Under 16.

Big Oz has told Patrick that he has a row of medals on his chest ('big chest') and that he is now 'a veteran.' Whereas Patrick and his friends are still only 'cadets.'

Patrick's team has done brilliantly at underage level and both Paula and I have derived great fun from watching these lads develop as footballers and friends.

They have benefitted from the guidance of excellent coaches the whole way up, I have to say.

Winning the League and Championship double in Grade 1 at Under 16 level has been the high point of these lads' achievements to date.

Patrick loves the Carrickmore pitch and having visited the Camp Nou stadium, he now reckons that Carrickmore's pitch and Barcelona's are the best two surfaces in the world.

That world is an absolutely perfect place when you are fifteen or sixteen and pull on your club jersey. Playing football with your friends... sure, how could you be bad to it?

I always listen closely when Jack and Joe offer wise counsel.

Barry Mc Elduff
Enjoyed connecting with cousins, uncles and aunts at last night's celebration in Loughmacrory marking Kevin and Patricia's 25th wedding anniversary. Uncles Jack and Joe offer wise counsel on the way forward for Sinn Féin and the future of Irish Republicanism.

Mobile Uploads · 29 August ·
View Full Size · Send as message · Report Photo

I like this photo of my two surviving uncles, Jack and Joe. You can see Jack's accompanying mug of tae in his hand as he and Joe hold court.

The occasion was the twenty-fifth wedding anniversary of cousin Kevin (nephew of Jack and Joe) and Patricia.

There was a marquee outside with food, drink and merriment all 'round but this conclave retreated to the sitting room inside to discuss affairs of the nation (not the same as state in the Irish context, come to think of it).

It was at a time when Unionist politicians were flipping the lid over the continued existence or otherwise of the IRA.

It was at a time when The Tories in the South of England threatened the very future of the political institutions which came about as a direct consequence of The Good Friday Agreement. They did this with their ideologically-driven attacks on low and middle-income families as well as our public services in the North of Ireland.

Jack and Joe are sages of a kind. They have been strong Republicans their whole lives.

It is now a documented historical fact that Jack (sometimes known as Danny) recruited Michael Gaughan from Mayo into the IRA in the early 1970s.

Like Frank Stagg, Michael died on hunger strike in an English Prison. Jack was very close to him.

For Joe's part, he once advised Sean South in the 1950s not to 'spook' the Volunteers at a training camp by making them say the rosary but instead to 'let the lads listen to Radio Luxemburg.'

Jack lives in Sligo and Joe in Dublin. Both have stuck with Sinn Féin all down the years through thick and thin.

Both are in their eighties now and both are intelligent thinkers.

I listened closely to my uncles at my cousin Kevin's house on that night in September as they offered wise counsel on the way forward.

Since that evening, Joe's beloved wife, Finola (née Coughlan) has passed away. Go nDéana Dia Trócaire uirthi.

It can all become too much
for some young people

Barry Mc Elduff
Late night sitting at Stormont became too much for these two Tyrone students, Jack and Gerard.

Barry Mc Elduff's photos in Mobile Uploads · 17 February ·
View Full Size

↪ Share

Many young people have gone on work experience with me in the past number of years.

They usually make contact with me directly themselves via email or by calling into our offices at John Street in Omagh. Then I have to fill out some forms and return them to the respective students' careers teachers / advisors   before confirming the travel and other arrangements.

I say 'travel' because Stormont is always the preferred setting for the young people as distinct from the constituency office which is more than interesting, too.

Early starts and late evenings are the order of the day when the students team up with me and I always try to offer them the optimum work experience.

I introduce them to inspirational people, they sit in on important meetings with me, they witness 'live' television or radio interviews as well as the plenary proceedings in the Assembly Chamber itself and they gain a real sense of the competing demands which an MLA or TD faces on a daily basis, balancing constituency and other pressures.

Teenagers and graduates tend to embrace the spirit of this experience.

There can, however, be one drawback: the cursèd late night Assembly sitting.

This tests the stamina of everyone, MLAs included. For the young person who waited outside the Patrician Hall in Carrickmore for me to collect them at 8am (or earlier) earlier that morning, midnight can come slow.

Their interest in the detail of the motion or piece of legislation being debated can wane and they might stretch themselves across two seats in the sanctuary of my office on the third floor.

It became too much for Jack McCallan (following in Oz ' footsteps) from Carrickmore and Gerard 'King of the Pool Table' from Omagh.

The two lads simply conked out.

Strong evidence that British Army structures remain intact

Barry Mc Elduff
I am struck by media attempts and newspaper advertising to promote the British Army as some kind of benign 'career.'
They'll call them 'Medical corps', 'Royal Irish', 'Highlanders' and 'Navy'. Call them as they are: British Army. And don't gloss over their murderous history in Ireland.

Barry Mc Elduff's photos in Mobile Uploads · 19 October · View Full Size

Reconciliation is a wonderful concept and it is very important in the context of conflict resolution and of shaping a better future for our country.

I am all for reconciliation between people in the North, between people North and South and between the people of 'these Islands'.

Personally speaking, however, one thing that is beyond reconciliation is any notion that the British Army should have any role or presence in Ireland, whether that be Limerick or Lisburn.

Irish Republicans are very creative and very positive. We take initiatives to breathe life into the peace process and political process. We compromise when it is appropriate to do so and we reach out.

But there is no glossing over the fact that the British Army has a malign history in Ireland and that there are only twenty-two countries in the world which they have not invaded.

The BBC might want to be jocular and jovial about 'our boys' but the vast majority of the people of Ireland do not believe that they are 'our boys.'

They have murdered 'our people' from Cork to Belfast and from Croke Park to Pomeroy.

It must be mighty to have a propaganda organ like the BBC or like ITV on your side.

How much focus did they apply to the recent incident in Ardglass when 'The Navy' (British Army) dragged a local fishing-boat under water and then pulled down the shutters and issued official denials ?

There is strong evidence to suggest that the command and operational structures of the British Army remain intact despite the development of the peace process.

Irish people are good at answering the call

Barry Mc Elduff

Pictured below is our recent white line picket held in Omagh in support of the people of Palestine who are being bombarded and murdered by the Israeli Government at this time.

A lot of people have contacted us to say that they would like the opportunity to participate in a solidarity protest because the last event was during a week day and they were not notified or able to attend because of work or other reasons.

On the one hand, the Irish are intrinsically very parochial as a people and as a nation, I would say. It always matters to us where someone is from. What village or town? What street or what townland?

I always let people define their own identity because there could be serious rivalry on the GAA front between where you think the person might be from and where they are actually from.

Some people say that they live in a particular area, like Coalisland or Loughmacrory but are from somewhere else, like Clonoe or Carrickmore. Two miles of difference can often be crucial in our mentality and frame of mind.

On the other hand, we can raise our game when we need to and show tremendous generosity whether that comes in the form of collecting aid for the people of Palestine or for those refugees trying their damnedest to flee Syria.

Individuals and community organisations respond quickly.

Sometimes, Sinn Féin fills the gap of local leadership and other times we weigh in behind the initiatives of others.

Quite often, the bin liners full of duvets, shoes, coats, toiletries and other essentials pile up in our offices at James Street in Omagh awaiting transportation to Belfast or Cork for onward transportation.

Sometimes, we organise white line pickets or attend candle-lit vigils organised by others in solidarity with persecuted people elsewhere in the world.

Social media has made the world an even smaller place and these platforms can be used to rally local support.

People are very good at answering the call.

SUSTAIN THE FLAME
Your health is your wealth

Barry Mc Elduff
In my MLA capacity, I will be attending a briefing meeting organised by The Western Health Trust on Friday morning. This briefing will apparently detail the financial position of The Western Health Trust at this time and also their 'savings plan'.

My concern going into this meeting is that changes or cuts to services at the Tyrone County Hospital in Omagh are being presented as 'agreed'. My question is; agreed by whom? Certainly not any elected Sinn Féin representatives for the area.

Already today I have met with Councillors Frankie Donnelly, Anne Marie Fitzgerald, Glenn Campbell, Barry McNally and Marty McColgan to discuss the detail of all of this.

Omagh lost our maternity services first, then our remaining acute services at the Tyrone County Hospital followed suit. Dungannon has also lost its acute services at the South Tyrone Hospital in recent times.

These experiences have been very stressful for local communities in rural Tyrone and this might explain why we are always on a high state of alert regarding any new threats to our health service locally.

As a West Tyrone MLA, I always prepare as best I can for quarterly meetings with senior managers of the Western Health Trust.

The type of issues that have exercised me in the past year include the disastrous decision to merge the palliative care ward (end-of-life care) with rehabilitation at the Tyrone County, and then the subsequent reduction in palliative care beds from ten to six.

They also include the future of acute mental health services in Omagh; the downgrading of the Addictions Treatment Unit (ATU) in Omagh; the need for new purpose-built health centres in Carrickmore and Fintona; the range of services that will be incorporated into the new Local Enhanced Hospital to meet the future needs of our community and also the reasons for any slippage in the timeline for delivering this project and also the closure of Dromore Day Care Centre. The latter was a bad, bad decision and I genuinely thought that our local efforts would save it.

When I visited the older people who used the Centre for respite and socialisation, one wee man whose shoes were polished jet black described the facility as 'a perfect place.'

One evening in September, I left a friend of mine who is a patient there back to Lime Ward at the Tyrone and Fermanagh Hospital. On the way there, he told me that the nursing staff were excellent but that the physical conditions were 'Dickensian.'

I resolved there and then to tackle this issue. We must 'cherish all the children of the nation equally' according to the 1916 Proclamation.

Calum and I sat at the Chairman's table

Barry Mc Elduff
Just come from afternoon with Institution of Civil
Engineers at Silverbirch Hotel in Omagh. Here, young
Calum Mathers addresses audience. Calum is a
Quantity Surveying student at Sligo IT. David Porter is
having excellent year as ICE Chairman and Aidan
O'Doherty made excellent address as Guest Speaker.

Barry Mc Elduff's photos in Mobile Uploads · 27 March ·

Young Calum Mathers impressed me the first time I met
him. He was working in his Granda's 'Hill Shop' on the
Kevlin Road in Omagh at the time, dividing his time
between school and his part-time job.

Calum had an easy manner and he dealt with customers
comfortably and confidently.

A year or two later, he told me that he was studying Civil Engineering in Sligo. When he told me this, I added two and two together and the result was four.

I said to him to put a particular date in his diary and to be my guest at the annual Institute of Civil Engineers Lunch held in The Silverbirch Hotel in the month of March.

This social event has become a 'must do' hardy annual for me as an MLA just like the Ulster GAA All-Stars Dinner organised by The Irish News every September in The Armagh City Hotel.

Anyway, Calum accepted my invitation and showed up on the day.

We sat at David Porter's table. David has enjoyed a very successful civil engineering career and was now a senior Director of The Rivers Agency.

It fell to me to formally welcome everyone to Omagh. I did this from the podium and before everyone tucked in to their lunch. All the big industry players were there, both public sector and private sector.

Calum needed a work placement later in the year as part of his degree course, so I decided to pitch for him in my short speech.

I explained that Calum was my guest at the event and I outlined his hopes for career progression. Then, I invited anyone who might be in a position to offer Calum a placement to come up to him over the lunch.

And they did precisely that.

Calum had brought along copies of his CV and he ended up with a pocket full of business cards as well as several follow-up lines of enquiry.

Calum worked the room like a true professional.

On leaving, he told me that he learned a lot that afternoon about how the world of networking works.

And the lunch wasn't bad either.

Meant to say 'best wishes' to a good friend of mine

Barry Mc Elduff

Meant to say 'best wishes' to a good friend of mine who is indeed 'a person of great integrity and who has worked very hard for Sinn Féin and for the people of Ireland over a very long time' : Bobby Storey. And the other lads, too, who are widely respected within Republican family: Eddie and Brian.

Barry Mc Elduff's photos in Mobile Uploads · 10 September ·

You would have to seriously ask why, in the month of September, the PSNI arrested Bobby Storey and three other Belfast Republicans who have worked hard to secure Republican buy-in to the peace and political process.

Maybe Peter Robinson or Mike Nesbitt could throw some light on this.

Bobby is someone I know very well. He is a man of considerable intellect and great integrity.

Every year, because big Bob or his friend, Bill Groves ask me to, I compere the Quiz Night in Andersonstown Social Club as part of Belfast's Féile an Phobail.

A couple of years ago, Bobby presented me with a statuette of Countess Markievicz because he reckoned I was 'one of the finest women in the Republican struggle.'

So, Bobby can be a jester and a messer, too.

He and I have collaborated in running the auction for Cairde Shinn Féin at their Annual Dinner in The Europa Hotel for several years, a sort of double act aimed at persuading the patrons with more of their cash than they might otherwise have planned to.

Bobby is often described as this or that in the media and is famous for the leadership role that he played in The Great Escape from The H Blocks of Long Kesh in 1983.

The Tyrone man in me needs to salute Seamus Campbell from Clonoe and all the other lads who escaped that day, too.

If the Brits had men like Bobby (or Seamus) in their ranks, they would probably award them an OBE or something.

I don't think that they will be offered any titles from the Brits anytime soon.

Bobby is like the public persona of a Movement which is made up of thousands of people. The majority of these people are low profile and want to remain so.

I know who I am talking about here and I salute them all, many of them in my own part of Tyrone.

Bobby is now the Chairman of Sinn Féin at Cúige level in the North.

As Bobby said to me one day in a private conversation about Republicans needing to change our tactics so as to actually win Irish freedom;

'The soldier has to go where the needs of the struggle are at. The struggle does not have to go where the needs of the soldier are at !'

Sometimes I think commentators want the whole thing to fail

 Barry Mc Elduff
Every time I see or hear the BBC and Irish News'
favourite Unionist commentator, Alex Kane, I get the
distinct impression that he wants failure more than
anything else in the world.

Barry Mc Elduff's photos in Mobile Uploads · 22 June ·

It is remarkable that none of the media people or
commentators who become politically involved ever join
Sinn Féin. Or is it ?

Many of those who report or read the news appear to have
political agendas themselves and this is sometimes boren out
by their subsequent career choices.

You have to look no further than Mike 'Soundbite' Nesbitt
of the UUP.

Fergal McKinney of the SDLP can't help showing a similar
type of disdain for Republicans and then, of course, in the
South, John Drennan is now a signed-up advisor to Lucinda
Creighton of Renua, that new, untested political outfit which
comes across as a sort of Fine Gael Light.

Of course, George Lee, once RTE's Economics Editor took time out to secure election as a Fine Gael TD in a by-election.

George only stayed the distance for a short while before beating a hasty retreat back to Donnybrook when he wasn't given the portfolio which he wanted.

Among the most negative and uninspiring of the local journalists who were formerly politically active simply has to be Alex Kane of the BBC and, inexplicably, The Irish News.

Kane was once 'Head of Communications' within the UUP... I wouldn't put that on my CV if I was him...and sometimes presents as the ultimate grim reaper and pessimist of the age. Kane seems to want everything to fail and he curses the plague on everybody's houses.

He would make you despair if you listened to him too often and he confers great nobility on non-voters.

Alex admires those who can't be bothered.

On the 'nationalist' side of things, I would commend the likes of Jude Collins, Danny Morrison and Chris Donnelly.

From Omagh originally, Jude Collins is a fantastic blogger and is a 'must read.' He interviewed me via the Periscope medium in my Stormont office earlier this year, revealing an ever-willingness to embrace new technology and new media despite his 'mature' stage of life.

Chris and Danny make strong contributions when called into action and it is always particularly good to see them warming up on the sideline.

Brian Feeney can be interesting and well-informed, too, of course, and he sometimes writes off the SDLP, the party to which he once belonged, whatever the story behind that is.

Some people say to me nowadays, 'You can imagine how impartial the news was when Mike Nesbitt used to read it.'

The people of Fintona saved their library

Barry Mc Elduff
Good to see major refurbishment of Fintona Library coming on well. People of Fintona stood up strongly for their library. Look forward to its re-opening.

Barry Mc Elduff's photos in Mobile Uploads · 21 May ·

Fintona Library looks really well and it is the most fantastic facility.

I was delighted to play my part in the campaign firstly to save the library in Fintona and then to secure major investment to refurbish it.

I don't want to exaggerate my involvement because the main role in this campaign was played by the local people in Fintona themselves.

Myself and Councillor Glenn Campbell always want to strongly represent the people as best we can but sometimes our presence in Fintona is more about facilitating the leadership of others within that community rather than competing for a place in the front row.

Fintona has had its fair share of social problems and sometimes sections of the local media appear to unduly highlight particular incidents when it really is a case of a small number of hoods attempting to hold everyone else to ransom.

The local magistrate was less than helpful with her comments on one occasion and I wrote to 'The Lord Chief Justice' to complain.

The Fintona I love to witness is the spirit of the people coming together to help prevent flooding, or the Pearses GAC presenting their club grounds in such a manner as to earn the respect of the whole county and even province.

I loved being there when the passion of the people shone through that night in The Golf Club.

Those senior 'Libraries NI' officials who carried out that public consultation were left with no uncertain understanding about the determination of the people to retain their library in the face of a proposal to close it.

Hundreds took part in a Colour Run in the town in early September this year to raise awareness of depression and to raise funds for the Aware charity.

Glenn told me about this wonderful initiative which was undertaken by young Megan Mullan and her friends.

More 'Mo Chara' than
Mo Farah, Sarah reckons

 Barry Mc Elduff
Just sayin ' ... like...a picture says more than a thousand
words.

Barry Mc Elduff's photos in Mobile Uploads · 14 September ·
View Full Size · Send as message · Report Photo

👍 Like   💬 Comment   ➤ Share

I owe @alice_liddell, I think, for this creative photo of me
ahead of the pack, including the world's top sprinters and
Usain Bolt himself.

You know me, if I say I ran the Tyrone Colour Marathon,
what I really mean is that I was part of a relay team with
Glenn Campbell and Stephen McCann and that I ran six
miles.

Still, in the spirit of me being a legend in my own mind (if
nobody else's), I derived great fun from this tweet which I

retweeted and then, having saved and stored the photo image, put it up as a Facebook post making the best of both platforms to bring more people into the craic.

I do get carried away a bit with my sporting imagination as I suggested earlier.

Ten out of ten also goes to Sarah Gallagher who commented that it was more a case of 'Mo chara' than it was of 'Mo Farah.'

However, my imagination is built on some wee foundation, I shall have you know, given that when I played for the Carrickmore senior football team, I used to win many of the sprints at training...except perhaps when Colm Harte was on top form, I should concede, in the interests of truth.

But then again, anybody would run fast if you knew that Raymond Munroe or Eamonn Loughran was running after you.

The intervening years and the struggle for liberation slowed me up a bit (what a man!) but running and playing football has never left my mind.

In the run up to a 5k or a 10k which I might have run a couple of years ago, I often used to joke that Stevie Duncan from Omagh 'will not sleep tonight if he hears that I am togging out tomorrow'.

I so admire strong local runners like Stevie, or like Dominic McCartan.

Some years ago I ran for half a mile through Omagh with the mighty Eamonn Coughlan before he, how shall I put it, left me at Scarffe's Entry.

Coughlan waited for me at the finishing line and greeted my return with, 'Where did you go ?'

Life is lived in the head, isn't it ?

The Crum featured in my first ever Fb post

 Barry Mc Elduff
I visited Crumlin Road Prison yesterday. Guided tour
was ok. Just wish they wouldn't ignore recent history.
Spent a while there myself as a political prisoner almost
25 years ago...both A Wing and C Wing. Harsh regime
but great community spirit among Republican prisoners.
KHL

Barry Mc Elduff's photos in Mobile Uploads · 30 July 2014 ·
View Full Size · Send as message · Report Photo

The first ever post that I put up was on 30 July 2014. It was
a picture of me visiting the Crumlin Road Prison in Belfast
that very day.

The visitor experience was handier, shall I say, than the prisoner experience.

I am not making myself out to be a hero or a martyr or anything like that when I say that 'I languished in a cell for Ireland' but I do use that phrase sometimes to wind up Paula as if I am looking for sympathy.

Another way of putting it is to say that I spent nine months on remand there, on twenty-three hours a day lock-up for nine months in 1991/1992.

Needless to say, I was there on a political charge, an age-old tradition in Ireland, you could say, and one that ran for sure in both my family's and Paula's.

A bit like having Championship medals.

If you are in the company of other former prisoners, you would nearly be embarrassed to say the length of time you were in because we have had plenty of our own Nelson Mandelas in Ireland. Thousands of people in this country have been jailed for political reasons down the centuries and not least in recent times.

In the Republican community, IRA prisoners wore a badge of honour.

In my Facebook post, I gently touched on this, even if the visit tour experience nowadays avoids the real story.

This post reached 10,036 people, received 16 comments and attracted 305 likes.

Thousands of politically motivated prisoners have passed through The Crum.

I met some characters and made good friends there.

Fighting elections is serious business

Barry Mc Elduff
Sinn Fein office in Omagh like busy exam centre with large team enveloping letters flat out urging voters to support Pat Doherty.

Mobile Uploads · 26 April ·
View Full Size · Send as message · Report Photo

Serious effort is put in by Sinn Féin activists who fight elections. So much so that for the most dedicated canvassers, normal living is virtually suspended for about six weeks.

Some ticket sellers for GAA clubs on a major 'once-in-every-five-years' fundraising drive would understand the type of intense commitment that is required over the period of a month or more.

Elections happen every couple of years at least and we go out to ask people directly, as much as possible, to vote for our candidates and for the Sinn Féin vision of Irish unity.

I tend to go out six days a week for six or seven weeks, taking the occasional evening out to recharge my batteries.

The most recent election we fought in West Tyrone was the Westminster one in May. This saw Pat Doherty returned as MP with a majority of over ten thousand votes.

Part of our formula for success is that we are out and about among our people all of the time and they don't just see us at election times.

We deploy a series of methods of community engagement all year 'round.

I always feel grateful to those who promote Sinn Féin in their local communities.

Enveloping thousands of letters to be posted to voters indiscriminately on a register might be one task best done in a socialising environment between friends.

You'd want a bit of craic while carrying out this otherwise mundane task.

Not everyone, however, appreciates a letter from Sinn Féin in the post. One man, describing himself as 'a Loyalist from the Hospital Road' rang the office to say never ever to write to him again.

But then he wouldn't tell us his name so that we could comply with his request and take his name off the register.

Two teams go to war every year

Barry Mc Elduff
Yesterday's Senior Tyrone County Hurling Final was a brilliant match with lethal effort put in by both teams. I have to say that the Carrickmore performance was mighty indeed, a real team effort full of committment and no small amount of skill. Great to see Damian Maguire lift the Benburb Cup.

The rivalry between Dungannon Eoghan Ruadh and Carrickmore Éire Óg is legendary and yesterday's match at Healy Park lived up to the billing. Like others, I went straight to Ballinamullan afterwards to see out Under 16 footballers beat Cappagh in the Championship. Between hurling and football yesterday, I hardly saw a bite. KHL.

Barry Mc Elduff's photos in Timeline Photos · 15 September 2014

Carrickmore and Dungannon have gone to war this year, and last year, and for several decades.

How otherwise would you describe the Tyrone County Hurling Final between the fiercest of rivals.

Last year, Damien Maguire lifted the Benburb Cup for Carrickmore Éire Ógs and this year, the honour fell to Brendan Begley.

This September's single-point win nudged Carrickmore one ahead in the county title stakes.

23 to Eoghan Rua's 22.

These are serious sportsmen who are not as recognised as their footballing brothers, neighbours or cousins in a football mad county, as you know.

But they deserve massive respect as do The Shamrocks, Naomh Colmcille and everyone who is actively involved in promoting hurling, Camogie and indeed handball.

I could say the same about boxing, running, cycling and other footballing codes as well because sport is intrinsically good.

But back to these hurling lads, some of whom are dual players.

Aidan Kelly scored the winning point in this year's County Final but that was no accident as I have seen him practising frees for years at Fr. McGilligan Park in Carrickmore.

As for Dungannon's Damien Casey, I just wonder how he would have fared had he been born in Kilkenny or Tipperary.

And when their war is over for a year, these boys, Grogans and Devlins among them, team up in common cause for their county, improving year on year.

The children of Sixmilecross
are trying to sleep

Barry Mc Elduff
People have the right to march and celebrate their 'culture' but I have to say that half past nine in Sixmilecross on a Wednesday night in September, night before school, is the wrong time. I have asked Parades Commission to pay more attention to late night parade notifications which come from Loyalist flute bands in Sixmilecross. I have to give voice to concerns of local residents.

Barry Mc Elduff's photos in Timeline Photos · 4 September 2014 ·

I raised the hare about this late night Loyalist parade in Sixmilecross because local people asked me to do this.

In keeping with the mood of the local people, my tone was constructive and I did not contest the principle of such a parade. Rather, I focussed on the time of night that it started and ended at, and also the fact that it was the night before the return to school for many children and young people, some of whom live in the Main Street.

You can see from the comments that it was a measured enough exchange on Facebook. This was my second ever post.

Sixmilecross is a place where there are good relations between the traditions, like Beragh and Fintona.

There is, however, some wee discomfort at the putting up of bunting and flags on the assumption that it is ok for Unionists to do this while God Forbid should the nationalists of that area ever decide to show their colours.

Tyrone GAA flags might be tolerated but the national flag of Ireland would probably be a step too far for those marching under the Union Jack while the Mothers and Fathers in the 'Cross were tucking in their little ones who would be starting P1 the next morning.

One comment queried why there were Scottish flags being carried in the parade because the Scots appear to be marching themselves to a different tune, that of Scottish Independence and the break-up of the Union as we all know it.

More recently, in the town of Fintona, the organisers of the Twelfth Parade there exhibited some respect for the local community by putting up their bunting the night before and taking them down again the next evening.

Ian Milne is another proud son of Bellaghy

Barry Mc Elduff added **2 new photos**.

13 July at 19:36 ·

Just back from Galbally where Ian Milne addressed Martin Hurson's 34th Anniversary commemoration. Great to meet many Republican stalwarts and members of Martin's clann there.

Ian Milne is a proud Bellaghy community man and a true son of South Derry. Perhaps more than anything else, Ian is a dedicated Irish Republican and a strong family man.

Ian's MLA office is two doors down from mine on the third floor of what is sometimes referred to as 'Stormont Parliament Buildings'.

I regularly call in to his office where Patricia calls the shots and where Ian pours himself a mug of tea and offers the rest of us one as well.

He drops by Room 338, too, most plenary days to compare notes on this and that.

The Derry Championship and The Tyrone Championship often feature. Ian's brother, Bobby won eight or nine Championship medals for Bellaghy and I suspect that Ian would have, too, had he been 'available'.

Ian and I sit together on the Statutory Committee for The Environment at Stormont which is chaired by Anna Lo.

Within the Sinn Féin team of three on the Committee, we confer leadership on Cathal Boylan from Keady because there is not much about the subject matter and the legislative process that Cathal doesn't know.

Ian has a tremendous interest in the legacy of the late poet laureate, Seamus Heaney and he has worked very hard to attract support and funding for a Centre in Heaney's honour in Bellaghy which, I am proud to say, is being built by Brendan Loughran & Sons from Carrickmore.

If I can take my own direction here, Ian has also a massive interest, probably reflecting his very essence, in the legacy of Francis Hughes and of Thomas McElwee. These two men were also proud sons of Bellaghy both of whom died on hunger strike in 1981.

Ian also languished in the H Blocks at the time as a political prisoner.

In the late seventies, the Brits put up 'Wanted' Posters of Ian, of Francis and of Dominic McGlinchey all over their native county and beyond. I can appreciate why.

One of the reasons might be that he was one of nineteen men who escaped from Portlaoise Prison in 1974. As the song goes:

'There's nineteen men a-missing and they didn't use the door, Just blew a little hole, where there wasn't one before...'

Today, Ian is an elected MLA with an enormous work rate and a vision of a free, united Ireland.

Twitter
@BarryMcElduff

'Ordinarily he was insane,
but he had lucid moments when he was merely stupid.'
Heinrich Heine

In this section, I have simply collated a selection of tweets from the first ten months of 2015 alone to share what floats my boat as far as Twitter is concerned.

I embraced Twitter quite some time before I took a look at this Facebook-thing and before I started to write my weekly blog.

In all, since I first tweeted, I have put out over five and a half thousand tweets.

Twitter certainly forces you to be succinct and to edit and abbreviate your thoughts. 140 characteristics concentrates the mind.

Regarding content, I have witnessed great examples of genius and wit on Twitter and I have also experienced bullies ganging up to quell legitimate freedom of speech.

Loyalists do not have a monopoly in this area but woe betide anyone who dares to assert their pride in being an Irish Republican. The softer but classic 'put down' is often to ask if you have nothing better to be doing with your time.

The world is ravaged with war and hunger and all you can do is to tweet.

Sometimes on Twitter, you might even feel threatened or at least frowned upon by trolls who are horrible and destructive.

'Trojan Shinner' is just one troll who is big into being obnoxious.

Sometimes I think that you would need body armour on Twitter.

Twitter is fast- moving, 'though and nobody hangs about.

Twitter can be more positive than negative, of course, and retweets are great for endorsing stuff coming out of the Dáil, for example, when Gerry Adams, Mary Lou, Caoimhghin and the team might have the Blueshirts or Mícheál Martin's crew on the run. Or other stuff not connected to politics and which maybe puts a smile on your face.

Barry McElduff MLA
@BarryMcElduff

Really enjoyed taking part in Guinness
World Record for most ever playing
Exhibition Gaelic Football match
#Drumragh

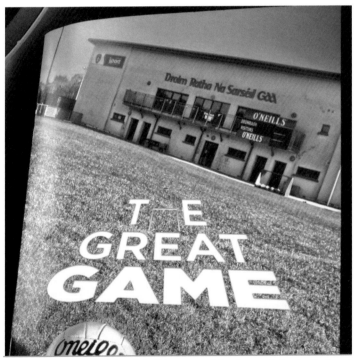

Drumragh Sarsfield's GAC is one of the best clubs in Ireland
when it comes to promoting participation and fun.

<   **Tweet**   🔍 ✍

🔁 Barry McElduff MLA Retweeted

Chris Curran
@CJCurran1

35 @TyroneGAALive Handballers are among 250 Irish bidding 4 @2015worlds gold medals in Canada tyronelife.com/tyronelifeblog…

👤 Barry McElduff MLA and 9 others
10/08/2015 17:06

<   **Tweet**   🔍 ✍

Barry McElduff MLA
@BarryMcElduff

Needed a wee 'Nitebite' before commencing evening canvass on the Derry Road in Omagh @PatDohertyMP

15/04/2015 17:23

Barry McElduff MLA
@BarryMcElduff

Nice to spend some time with relatives and neighbours at last night's event to say 'Slán' to Omagh District Council.

28/03/2015 14:50

Barry McElduff MLA
@BarryMcElduff

These are Patrick's Under 16 Championship and League medals. Great year for An Charraig Mhor !

Barry McElduff MLA
@BarryMcElduff

Bit late for tweet but Rossa does Strictly unbelievably well. Jane Adams and I think we won.

Barry McElduff MLA
@BarryMcElduff

Carrickmore goalie, Big Oz got injured after postal deadline. Now walking to polling station. Refused all lift offers

Barry McElduff MLA
@BarryMcElduff

2 types of Tayto in Ireland.
Any need?
Which do you prefer?
RT for @MrTaytoIreland (red)
FAV for @MrTaytoNI (yellow)

10/02/2015 15:06

... you will be interested to know that the Free State Tayto won the public vote. This question might now feature in a future United Ireland referendum. :)

Barry McElduff MLA
@BarryMcElduff

To get my Snickers, I have to go deep into DUP territory on Stormont's Third Floor. No vending machine on SF side.

Ulster Herald
@Ulster_Herald

Long wait ends as Trillick crowned as champions - ulsterherald.com/2015/10/11/lon...

11/10/2015, 22:08

Barry McElduff MLA
@BarryMcElduff

Declan lost selfie stick but still managed to capture SF4 for Assembly at Pat Doherty's MP election launch in Omagh.

21/03/2015 14:37

4 RETWEETS **3** FAVORITES

... Declan, Grace, Michaela and I go before the electorate in May 2016, le cuidiú Dé #StandingUp4WestTyrone

Tweet

Barry McElduff MLA
@BarryMcElduff

Trying to figure out where to place this statue of Peter in Room 338 in Stormont.

10/03/2015 13:34

3 RETWEETS **8** FAVORITES

Some Armagh supporters made very unkind suggestions as to where I should place this statue of the Errigal Ciaran man.

Barry McElduff MLA
@BarryMcElduff

With cousin (Cllr) Ann Marie, Uncle Joe, Caoimhghin O Caolain TD and Martin Ferris TD during break in Ard Fheis.

07/03/2015 15:46

Barry McElduff MLA
@BarryMcElduff

Pleased today to wish Liam O'Neill every future success in the week when he steps down as GAA President.

23/02/2015 17:15 from Dublin City, Ireland

🔁 Barry McElduff MLA Retweeted

Ryan McAleer
@RyanMcAleerUH

Film on Omagh man Donal Donnely's epic 1960 jail escape starting 10.15pm on @RTEOne - ulsterherald.com/2015/09/15/rte…

15/09/2015 22:13

Barry McElduff MLA
@BarryMcElduff

Congrats to Megan Mullan. Hugely successful colour run in Fintona 4 BEAT charity. Cllr Glenn Campbell & Leona in pic.

The Irish Times ✓
@IrishTimes

Kenny should intervene directly on plight of Travellers, says Adams irishtimes.com/news/ireland/i...

20/10/2015, 22:19

@GerryAdamsSF calling on people to #rocktheloch tomorrow night 🎵🎸🔊🇮🇪

Gerry Adams is a great man for Twitter - with nearly 10,000 tweets under his belt and over 90,000 followers. His messages deal with serious issues and sometimes not so serious, both national and local. @GerryAdamsSF
Martin and Mary Lou are also adept at Twitter, fair play to them.

MLAs And The Like
@MLAsAndTheLike

Under the Executive d'Hondt rules, Barry McElduff replaces Arlene as the new Minister for Pointing at Things

11/09/2015 19:11

28 RETWEETS **25** FAVORITES

Have you ever noticed how politicians always point at things in photographs. Sometimes potholes, some sometimes iPhones.

Tweet

↻ Barry McElduff MLA Retweeted

Pat Spillan
@dabollix

Stormont In Disarray As McElduff Starts Swinging At Nesbitt Over HP Sauce. Maskey On... tyronetribulations.com/2015/09/10/sto...

10/09/2015 20:21

24 RETWEETS **17** FAVORITES

I was at a Sinn Féin meeting in Drogheda when Martin McGuinness drew my attention to this humourous tweet.

Barry McElduff MLA
@BarryMcElduff

Sandwiches packed. Diesel fill in Emyvale.
Toll paid. Breakfast @ Applegreen. Clonliffe
College Car Park. Wet. Early.

↻ Barry McElduff MLA Retweeted

Barry McColgan
@BarryMcColgan

That awkward moment when the British
Embassy re-opens on Bobby Sands'
Street, Tehran.

21/08/2015 16:22

203 RETWEETS **151** FAVORITES

Tweet

13 Barry McElduff MLA Retweeted

Sinn Féin ✓
@sinnfeinireland

One cannot defend the poor but can spend £500m on Faslane Trident base
@BarryMcElduff

"George Osborne has made a nonsense of his own claims there is no more money to pay for protections for the most vulnerable people in our society and public services by pledging £500 million for the upgrade of a nuclear submarine base at Faslane.

"It is grotesque that the Tory cabinet of millionaires thinks this is an acceptable use of public money while tens of thousands are being driven deeper into poverty."

Barry McElduff MLA

@BarryMcElduff

02/09/2015 17:13

29 RETWEETS **19** FAVORITES

Thanks to David and Michael in our Press Office for coming up with this Nuclear Submarine image to enhance my message.

t⟲ Barry McElduff MLA Retweeted

Catherine Kelly
@sanepolitico

Shocked?well you should be at the sight of
a Libyan mother trying to keep her baby
from drowning. Reject xenophobia!

28/08/2015 18:41

311 RETWEETS **120** FAVORITES

We all need to open our hearts and our doors to the refugees.
Well said, Catherine.

Tweet

🔍 ✍

↻ Barry McElduff MLA Retweeted

Phil Flanagan
@PhilFlanagan

The irony of British people complaining about an 'immigration crisis.' There are only 22 countries they never invaded

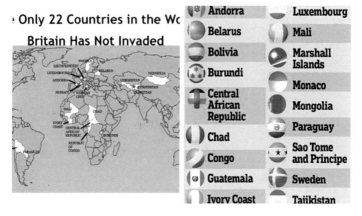

27/08/2015 10:48

ıll VIEW TWEET ACTIVITY

12 RETWEETS **15** FAVORITES

'If you see two fish fighting in a pond, you know that the British have been there beforehand' - a saying from Sierra Leone. Flanagan the man.

⟲ Barry McElduff MLA Retweeted

O'Neills
@ONeills1918

Tyrone jerseys are made in Tyrone for Tyrone by Tyrone people in Strabane. County store: goo.gl/RpfZ3A #GAA

21/08/2015 20:30

19 RETWEETS **29** FAVORITES

I was amazed to see how many people work at O'Neill's in Strabane #HomeGrownSuccess

↻ Barry McElduff MLA Retweeted

Teamtalkmag.com
@teamtalkmagLIVE

Teamtalk Radio back on the road today in Coalisland. No need for a press box on a day like this #TTMagRadio #Coverage

16/08/2015 16:31

3 RETWEETS **8** FAVORITES

Noel McGinn and the team keep us updated week in, week out.

↻ Barry McElduff MLA Retweeted

Gaelic Life
@Gaelic_Life

THE SQUID - A new injury-treatment product that combines compression and cold therapy - gaeliclife.com/2015/08/the-sq…

"Personal Health & Fitness" is always a step ahead in helping people to get fit and to recover from injury. Damien Crowne ahead of the game.

Barry McElduff MLA
@BarryMcElduff

No better man than SF Councillor Stephen McCann to be elected chair of Fermanagh and Omagh Health Group for 2015/2016

10/08/2015 19:04

2 RETWEETS **11** FAVORITES

McCann had the great honour of piping the Trillick Team up the street after they won the County Final.

Barry McElduff MLA
@BarryMcElduff

Looking good in Omagh town centre tonight. PRIMARK opens in September, I hear. Good for retail choice in town centre.

Great to see the big stores but be sure to visit the smaller shops when you are in the town.

< **Tweet**

Barry McElduff MLA
@BarryMcElduff

I hear that Aaron McCann was 'class' in the Strule Arts Centre in Omagh over the weekend.

22/06/2015 21:12

< **Tweet**

Barry McElduff MLA
@BarryMcElduff

Disappointed that Irish National Flag not flying over Stormont today. I think it should be flown more often #equality

04/06/2015 10:36

Blogs
extracts 2015
tyronemansblog.wordpress.com

'The future is here.
It's just not widely distributed yet'.
William Gibson
author of Neuromancer; the originator of the term "cyberspace" in 1984

If you take fifteen minutes out every day to write two hundred words, and if you take one day off every week, before you know it, you will become a weekly blogger.

That is if you don't mind sharing your views and observations online with half the country or with whomever might be interested.

I put my blog up on Facebook and on Twitter usually around midday on a Friday. Often it amounts to twelve hundred words or so. In many ways, your blog is the modern-day equivalent of the old-style, conventional journal or diary that some used to keep.

Commitment, consistency and discipline are three things that are required. You know what one definition of commitment is: it is when you are still doing what you said you would do long after the initial feeling of enthusiasm has left you.

My blog is embellished by photographs and images. Few want to read voluminous print in this day and age so you have to make things more appealing to the eye.

My blog covers many topics: from the progress of Carrickmore Under 16s to political debates on the Hill; from dead sheep lodged in the weir of the River Strule to the CDs to which I listen while driving through the night.

I find this therapeutic and I enjoy the feedback. Plus, to put it simply, a painter must paint, a writer must write and a corner forward must score goals and points.

What you can be, you must be.

tyronemansblog

January

Not every day you carry the National Flag into Ballymena Town Hall

Did you know that I addressed the inaugural meeting of the North Antrim Roger Casement Ógra Sinn Féin Cumann. This meeting was held in Ballymena's beautiful civic building, The Braid, effectively the modern version of Ballymena Town Hall.

I wish the Cumann every success for the future and I must say that it had to be at least a wee bit historic to be carrying our national flag into and out of Ballymena Town Hall. Don't ye think?

I told Sean Lynch to tell Ronnie that I was asking about him

Sean Lynch sent me a text over the New Year period to wish me all the best in 2015. The Fermanagh MLA was texting me from South Africa where he had just teamed up again with the former Head of the ANC's military wing, Ronnie Kasrils.

I met Ronnie myself one time in a rural part of Tyrone so I told Sean to tell Ronnie that I was asking about him.

Delivering the message on behalf of our teachers and parents

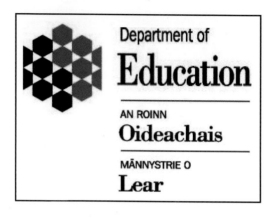

I promised many teachers, parents and classroom assistants that I would personally hand deliver their lobbying letters regarding the Draft Education Budget.

The deadline for the receipt of submissions was Monday 29 December. So I drove to Bangor that very day and left off a sack full of letters with a representative of the Minister's Private Office.

I am on the side of our school communities and I reasonably expect that the Executive will do all in its power to support John O'Dowd and his Department. The stakes are very high and I think that the Education Budget should be protected in the same way that the Health Budget is protected.

Sinn Féin supports this even when the Minister is a DUP Minister. Of course, the elephant in the room is the British Tory party which is trying to choke our Executive of necessary resources to do its job.

I do not subscribe to the notion that Britain 'subsidises' us in a benign fashion, a British Government which refuses to tell us how much tax they take from Ireland and which is slow to transfer to us revenue raising levers.

Racists always welcome in the British Army

The Tyrone Times newspaper tells us this week that a 23 year old man from the Bush area was found guilty at Dungannon Magistrates Court of an 'explicitly racist' attack in the town. The man in question was part of a large gang who assaulted and gave chase to three men who have come to live and work here.

In his defence, the man's barrister said that he has now joined 'the Army Reserves' and that this will provide him with 'the backbone and stability that he needs'.

I presume that the barrister was talking about the British Army. You see, I always think of the IRA when I hear the term, 'the Army'.

The Dungannon man who was convicted should feel very at home in the British Army. It sounds to me as if he possesses all of the entry requirements and characteristics that the Brits are looking for.

They are made for each other.

Republicanism and gaelic football rhymed for Patsy

I always struggle with the idea of writing in my blog about someone who has just died. But I do need to say something about Patsy McGarvey from Castlederg who died last weekend and who was buried on Thursday of this week.

There has been a lot said about Patsy this week. He had a big heart, he was a stalwart Irish Republican and he was generous to a fault in the same way that the late Cathal Quinn from Dromore was generous to a fault.

Patsy had a big personality and we all came together this week to pay our respects and to remember him.

Pat Doherty MP spoke at Patsy's graveside and he said that Patsy was proud of every member of his family and that this distinguished McGarvey includes Patsy's brother, Ciaran McGarvey who lined out at full back for Tyrone in the 1980s.

Forgive me for straying now and telling you that at Patsy's wake, I asked Ciaran who was the best man he ever marked. Remember, Ciaran has marked Eoin Liston, The Bomber himself. You might think that I should not have asked Ciaran this question when sympathising with him and his brother, Gerard but I cannot help myself in these moments.

Without hesitation Ciaran named Matt Connor of Offaly whom he marked in The Centenary Cup at O'Neill Park in Dungannon.

Ciaran listened to lots of advice from Art McRory about how to handle the genius of Matt Connor but when it came to the practical, Ciaran's best intentions and Art's advice were to no avail. Matt destroyed him on the day.

I really should seek forgiveness for straying from writing directly about Patsy but in Tyrone, we just love it when Republicanism and gaelic football rhyme.

I touched on a great story in my book about the day Patsy accompanied me to Dregish Chapel to address people coming out of Mass, the Sunday before an election and when our PA system broke down on the way over.

I should have known that Patsy would win over the hearts of his neighbours without a PA and that is exactly what he did in the ensuing half hour. Patsy brought a smile to the faces of everyone who shook our hands on the way out of Dregish Chapel that day.

Go ndeana Dia trócaire ar a anam úasal agus mo chomh bhrón lena mhuintir.

tyronemansblog

February

You might appear calm but there could be a lot going on behind scenes

I was genuinely running from pillar to post in Stormont the other day. I was supposed to be here and I was supposed to be there and on top of these, there was now a delegation waiting for me in The Great Hall at the same time.

But I was meant to be in the Chamber for The Commencement Order of the Transfer of Planning Functions to Local Government. I needed to be there as well because Cathal Boylan was preoccupied in a meeting upstairs, which I had just abandoned myself, and he would normally handle this for us in the Chamber.

So, I appeared via a side door just at the point when Pam Cameron, a DUP MLA was concluding her remarks on the

Legislation being tabled before us. At that point, it struck me that my name may very well be called soon by The Speaker, that is, if our Party Whip had submitted my name to speak on behalf of Sinn Féin. Sometimes this happens without you actually knowing.

Seconds later I was called to rise in my place by Deputy Speaker John Dallat to address the issues. As I rose to my feet, I had three buss words in my head.

'Strategic', 'flexibility' and 'HR' as in Human Resources. I built my three main points around these three key words and sat down again without anyone noticing that I had nearly been caught cold. Phew…oh aye, and that is right, I then had to run to the front steps to meet and greet some students from St Mary's University College.

Young Ryan McAnespie played well against Tyrone, too well

It would have been a very proud moment for the McAnespie family when young Ryan stepped out for the Monaghan senior team last Saturday evening at Healy Park in Omagh.

Dessie Mone has praised the contribution that Ryan made to the Monaghan team on the evening which beat Tyrone in our opening match of the 2015 National Football League.

I know the McAnespie family quite well and cousins of theirs are cousins of mine, if you can figure that one out.

Ryan's sisters and mother, Brenda have starred for Monaghan Ladies and other members of the clann have lined out variously for Tyrone…once again, if you can figure this out.

I spent a lovely evening with Ryan's grandfather, John in Aughnacloy not so long ago when I brought Weeshie Fogarty of Radio Kerry fame to meet him on the evening of the 25th anniversary of Aidan, Ryan's uncle and John's son who was murdered by the British Army at the Aughnacloy checkpoint.

Ryan's father, Vincent has always been a sound Republican and so, too, have other members of the McAnespie clann. His mother was a Sinn Féin Councillor.

I was there in Healy Park last Saturday evening and was, of course, supporting Tyrone but I will confess to feeling good for the McAnespies when young Ryan made his senior debut at this level.

Raymond McCreesh every bit as heroic as 1916 Leaders

I see that Newry and Mourne Council have stood over their decision to name a play park after Hunger Striker Raymond McCreesh. And why wouldn't they?

Raymond McCreesh was no terrorist. He came from one of the most highly respected families in South Armagh and for me, as a teenager, and for many thousands of others, Raymond McCreesh was a hero and a martyr. Raymond McCreesh fought and died for Ireland and the Irish people.

Raymond McCreesh died on hunger strike. The level of his commitment and sacrifice is difficult to comprehend. I attended Raymond McCreesh's funeral. As a pupil at Omagh CBS, I often handed notes to teachers explaining why I had been absent the previous day.

I was very proud that my mother signed off on these notes which explained that I had been in attendance at the funeral of the latest Hunger Striker. When I studied at Queen's University, there were students in my year from South Armagh. Invariably, they were proud of the fact that Raymond McCreesh was one of theirs. Just as we were proud in Tyrone that Martin Hurson was one of ours.

Next year, people will be tripping over themselves to honour the men and women of 1916. For me, Raymond McCreesh and his comrades who died on hunger strike are every bit as heroic as the signatories of the 1916 Proclamation.

There are Irish people in possession of Nobel Prizes for their various contributions. As far as I am concerned, Raymond McCreesh would be more deserving of international recognition than many of the past recipients.

Go ndeana Dia trócaire ar a n-anamacha uaisle uilig.

Not only are we not ashamed, but we are very proud, in fact

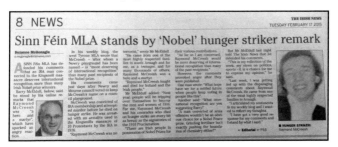

My simple tribute to Raymond McCreesh in last Friday's blog travelled a bit in the past week, further than I ever would have thought.

The News Letter was outraged. TalkBack brought Tom Elliot on to debate this with me in the BBC's Basement Studio at Stormont while Tracey Magee of UTV wanted to do a 'piece to camera' in The Great Hall for the evening news.

The Irish News contacted me to see if I was happy to stand over my remarks and Willie Frazer was uploading a video condemning me.

I kept thinking of the families of Ireland's Patriot Dead and how they deserve respect and support. I am proud to offer both.

A professional gentleman from a rural part of Tyrone rang me to say that not only was he not ashamed of Raymond McCreesh, but, in fact, he was very proud of him.

Lucky I had this letter in my pocket to put O'Donovan in his box

It is not often that I quote the Commissioner of An Garda Síochána to bolster my argument in a debate. But this is precisely what I had to do on Monday in the Seanad Chamber when Limerick Fine Gael TD and general upstart, Patrick O'Donovan accused Sinn Féin of benefiting from the proceeds of fuel laundering by the IRA.

Lucky I just happened to have in my pocket a letter signed by Superintendent Frank Walsh, Private Secretary to the Commissioner which stated that An Garda Síochána 'hold no information or intelligence to support the assertion' that the IRA is involved in fuel laundering, cigarette-smuggling and counterfeiting.

I read this out to the assembled parliamentarians in the Chamber and it had the required effect of nailing O'Donovan's untruth. Later the same evening, on RTE's Six

One News, David Davin Power made a reference to the fact that the letter 'appears to exonerate the IRA.'

I should say that the letter I produced was a letter from An Garda Síochána to Donegal North East TD, Padraig MacLochlainn.

Had to hear it directly from An Taoiseach himself

Some weeks ago I wrote to An Taoiseach asking him for a private meeting to discuss the A5 Road project.

Essentially, I wanted An Taoiseach to re-pledge his commitment to this hugely important road to opportunity in the greater north-west of Ireland.

Enda did agree to meet me on the fringe of the British Irish Parliamentary Assembly in Dublin on Monday morning last. In fairness, he did provide the commitment that I sought and this was further backed up by Transport Minister Paschal O 'Donohue TD.

He told me that 'some roads have a greater political status than others' and that the A5 remains a priority for the Government in Dublin just as it does for the administration at Stormont.

tyronemansblog

March

Nally himself a former prisoner

I hosted twelve former Political Prisoner from Derry last weekend. I was proud to show off our Garden of Remembrance and The Nally Stand. When I refreshed my knowledge of Pat Nally himself from County Mayo, I was reminded that this one and same Mr Nally was a former political prisoner himself and died in prison in 1891.

I think The Nally Stand Heritage Centre in Carrickmore contains great potential for the future. We need a space where we can tell our story. I enjoyed sitting around talking to Gerry McCartney and the rest of the lads against the backdrop of Joe McGarrity's image.

I don't always agree with people who say that sport and politics don't mix. Very often, they do and this is nowhere more apparent than in the evolution of the GAA.

Some even swell their chest with pride at not knowing

The worst illiterate is the political illiterate. He hears nothing, sees nothing, takes no part in political life. He doesn't seem to know that the cost of living, the price of beans, of flour, of rent, of medicines, all depend on political decisions. He even prides himself on his political ignorance, sticks out his chest and says he hates politics. He doesn't know, the imbecile, that from his political non-participation comes the prostitute, the abandoned child, the robber and, worst of all, corrupt officials, the lackeys of exploitative multinational corporations.
~ Bertolt Brecht

Some weeks ago, I wrote about a gentleman in Omagh who 'swelled with pride' when brushing me off that he had no interest in Gaelic football or politics. I had been visiting houses in the Tamlaght Road area at the time and I had asked the man to update me on an important match which was on TG4.

Then, I had asked him to accept a letter which gave him my contact details…"If you ever need to contact me as an MLA". It was at this point that the gentleman said that he had no interest in politics either.

After this experience, Barry McColgan sent me a text which detailed the following quote from Bertold Brecht:

"The worst illiterate is the political illiterate, he doesn't hear, doesn't speak, nor participates in the political events. He doesn't know the cost of life, the price of the beans, the fish, the flour, the rent, the shoes and the medicine, all depend on the political decisions. The political illiterate is so stupid that he is proud and swells his chest saying that he hates politics. The imbecile doesn't know that, from his political ignorance is born the prostitute the abandoned child, and the worst of all thieves, the bad and corrupted politician, lackey of the national and multinational companies."

A little harsh perhaps, do you reckon? Still, it is a class quote and one I intend to reuse if or when I encounter people who are proud of their disinterest and lack of concern which doesn't impress me much.

My friend was put on a plane and sent home

I was on the phone quite a bit this week to the United States. Someone I know was being detained in a 'Correctional Facility' over there pending deportation back home. He had been there four weeks. I have also been in regular contact with the young man's family on this side of the Atlantic. Understandably, they were very anxious about their family member's imprisonment and future uncertainty. The young man in question is hard working and paid his taxes. He had been in America ten years when detained. Unfortunately, in the last 24 hours, the young man was put on a plane and sent home. There are thousands of Irish people in this type of limbo. It is high time that the plight of the undocumented Irish was resolved.

Giving ALL children the best possible start in life

I turned my attention this week to the range of support services which are available to parents and children. Mothers who cannot benefit from SureStart courses are understandably anxious to secure access to such support. The problem is that only those who live in 'wards' of highest social deprivation can benefit from these services and very often very needy and deserving families lose out. I know budgets are incredibly tight but I have asked Minister John O'Dowd to begin a serious discussion within the Executive to see how best we can 'cherish all of the children equally' and truly give them the best possible start in life.

Earlier in the week at Stormont, Michaela Boyle and I hosted Winnie Kelly, SureStart Manager in Omagh and Rosemary Mullin, Speech and Language Support Worker. These women are experts in the field and know what they are talking about.

We met Junior Ministers Jennifer McCann and Jonathan Bell and made the case as best we could. In fairness, John O'Dowd has recently expanded SureStart access and now more people can benefit.   I will still explore the issue of universal access because I am listening to local people who are losing out and whose children are losing out.

The Trillick row even spilled over to the women at the bazaar

I called to see Peter Kelly in the townland of Golan on Sunday evening past. Peter and his wife, Pauline. Peter is a retiring Sinn Fein Councillor who is in his 79th year and presently recovering from a stroke. Stephen McCann is effectively Peter's successor and he joined me in paying a visit to see Peter. When I was leaving to go to a meeting in Trillick itself an hour or so after I arrived, I thought of a great quote from Steve Jobs; 'I would trade all of my technology for an afternoon with Socrates.'

What I am saying is that in a busy, busy world, there is real wealth in taking an hour out to speak with and listen to a man like Peter Kelly. Peter has seen a lot in his lifetime, including the murder of his beloved brother, Patsy by the UDR. Patsy was himself a highly respected Councillor before Peter's time. I particularly liked his reminiscences about a parish league in his youth when things got out of hand and ended up in rows between women at the local bazaar. I think the four teams were: Liffer, Golan, Lisdoo and Trillick (Town).

I should not comment any further on this internal Trillick stuff or take sides because Sean Donnelly, Seamus Gormley and The Kelly twins might be readers of my blog and might come knocking.

tyronemansblog

March

My grandfather and Charlie Daly were very great – Tyrone and Kerry united as one. My thoughts on Easter.

Easter is the most important time of the year as far as I am concerned. As Republicans, we remember our patriot dead and re-commit ourselves to the cause of bringing about the United Ireland for which so many gave their lives in many generations. This year, I will attend the Tyrone County Commemoration in Carrickmore on Easter Sunday evening and I will address commemorations both in Drumragh Graveyard, just outside Omagh and in Enniscorthy,

Co.Wexford not for the first time, I might add. I also have a speaking engagement in Ardoyne on Easter Tuesday and I will attend a talk in The Tyrone GAA Centre on Saturday evening at Garvaghey on the life of Kerry Republican, Charlie Daly, a close friend and comrade of my grandfather, James McElduff whom I am proud to say was himself a dedicated IRA Volunteer.

When I was showing strong interest myself during my teenage years, my Father used to say that I was 'worse than your GrandFather ever was' and I took this as the ultimate compliment I must say. Some of the combined efforts of my Granda and of Charlie Daly are chronicled in a book written by Uinseann Mac Eoin called, 'Survivors.' Meanwhile , connecting us up to the most recent generation of Volunteers, Paula will attend to the grave of her only and beloved brother, Patrick, as she does every year in Edendork.

I personally knew and was close to many of those who died in the conflict. I played football with some of them. I went to University with some of them and I tried to advance Irish Republicanism alongside many of them. This Easter we should pledge to live for Ireland, the ending of partition and the freedom of our country. I am very proud of everyone whose name appears on the Roll of Honour.
Thug siad an méid a bhi ina gcnámha.

From Dromore to Kenya, Ann Quinn is always on the go

In a Belfast Telegraph interview one time, I named 'The Salt and Pepper' in Dromore as one of my favourite restaurants. I said at the time that Gerry McKernan and his staff always served up a mighty feed at a great price. Sitting in The Salt and Pepper with Ann Quinn on a Saturday afternoon is quite an experience, it has to be said. Ann knows everybody and everybody's story. Everybody knows Red Ann. One minute, she is enquiring about their cataracts, the next she is commenting on the success of 'Same Old Moon' by the local St. Dympna's Drama Society.

Ann is no longer a Councillor, she tells the people, but they pay no heed to that and they confide in her anyway. Ann did not stand for the new Fermanagh and Omagh District Council but instead bowed out when Omagh District

Council was officially wound up at the end of March. This is only of academic importance, however, because Ann will always be a Councillor in Dromore.

Still, they ask her to come out and look at the overgrown hedges at the road junction and could she bring out a postal / proxy vote application form for their Mother when she is coming out. Ann makes a big saucepan of soup for Tummery Athletic on a Saturday and 'feeds the sows out of the same saucepan throughout the rest of the week,' she jokes as if this was something people did years ago. As I was saying, it is some experience being in The Salt and Pepper with Ann Quinn on a Saturday.

And i didn't even mention the charity work that Ann undertakes to help children in Africa. Perhaps another time…

Life in McCallan household
always a drama.

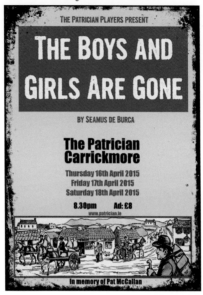

Last Saturday night, I attended a three-act play in Carrickmore performed by the local Patrician Players and directed by Declan Forde. 'The Boys And Girls Are Gone' by Seamus de Burca was the play chosen by the family of the late Pat McCallan from Striff as a tribute to Pat and indeed as a celebration of his life treading the boards. 'A good old Irish play performed on the stage of his beloved Patrician Hall,' was how Pat's wife, Tessie and their daughters explained it in the programme.

The cast of nine included four of Pat's own family. Two of Pat's daughters and two of his grandchildren. Emigration was one of the many themes but there so much more in it about people's lives in 'Kiltiernan,' including dowries, arranged marriages, domination and narrowness of mind.

In real life, I think very highly of Pat's daughter, Mary (McElduff) but for a couple of hours I was lost in this play and didn't care too much for 'Mrs Margaret Nowlan' or her harsh nature. Mary is definitely a chip of the old block. Hard to beat a good Irish play as the McCallan women said and what an appropriate way to honour Pat. I know, too, that I enjoyed thoroughly meeting up with many local people at the play. I did my rounds as you might imagine in the Hall because I knew everybody in the place.

I was also pleased to see a photo of Dan Gallagher, my uncle-in-law, in the programme and to see reference to the other Pat ('McGlynn') as well in a piece written by Roisin Hood of Creggan Drama Circle, entitled 'The Two Pats.' Three great actors from this community who were much loved and are still badly missed

tyronemansblog

May

Imagine being stopped by this nice law enforcing gentleman

On my way home from Kilkenny, I was called 'a Fenian Bastard' in the Applegreen Service Station at Lusk, just south of Drogheda. An oul codger with a pot belly, grey sideburns and a dark wig was the offending party. He was wearing a blazer and a tie with a crown symbol on it. He had a Belfast accent and was part of a group heading towards the bus after a pit stop at the Applegreen on their way home from Dublin.

He concluded his mouthing with a rude hand gesture and vamped out of the shop. Joe Gallagher and I didn't even ignore the ass-hole. He was an ex-something, possibly RUC or UDR or Prison Officer. I could tell. Shows you the calibre of individual we had in the North and who were masquerading as 'law.' If I had wanted to wind him up, I could have said, 'We haven't gone away, you know.' He was probably the nuisance on the bus with a half bottle of whiskey in him, Joe surmised, before adding that Joe himself was called many's a name in his working career as a teacher and a bouncer.

I recounted the experience to a group of Tyrone hurling supporters from Dungannon in 'The Applegreen' and they had unkind descriptions for the same gentleman, too, as you might imagine.At least Tyrone beat Fingal in the hurling.

Stephen, Roy and I
could be flying out together

Noel McAdam, Political Correspondent with The Belfast Telegraph rang me on Wednesday evening. He said that I had provoked the ire of Unionists with my response to a tweet from comedian, Tim McGarry. Tim had tweeted; 'Scrap the Assembly, let #FIFA run Northern Ireland. They certainly know how to raise funds.' To which I replied; ' Scrap 'NI' maybe. United Ireland only chance we have.' The DUP's Stephen Moutray and the UUP's Roy Beggs were said to be rippin'.

So they fired a few stones at me and called me a few names. My comments were 'badly timed' and 'irresponsible.' The cheek of me.

I was invited by Noel to reply because Noel and his paper love a good row. I did reply along the lines that at least Stephen, Roy and I have electoral mandates in this part of Ireland, unlike English Tory David Cameron who has none. In fact, I suggested that the three of us should unite as one team in opposition to Cameron. For it is he who is our real enemy. What he has in mind for our people, those who elect us is stark indeed. We could fly over together, the three of us, to London from Belfast City Airport. We'd have to bring photo ID, in my case, my passport.

tyronemansblog

June

Young fellows like Jude Collins know all about new technology

'Periscope' is a relatively new word which features in the lexicon of social media. Not everyone knows what it means and until Monday of this week, I really only associated it with whiz kids like Mairtín Ó Muilleoir @newbelfast. The South Belfast MLA is 'living the dream' and runs the corridors of Stormont videoing all before him in the interests of accountability and transparency.

Then respected commentator and writer, Jude Collins invited me to be interviewed on Periscope about the current political situation and my recent 'controversial' suggestion that 'NI' should be scrapped. This was in response to Tim McGarry's idea of scrapping the Assembly and letting FIFA run the Six Counties. Now I was about to find out all about the latest version of periscope. I said 'no problem' to Jude and so he joined me at Stormont.

He duly set up his tripod for holding his mobile in place and then trained its video camera on me. Jude did one final check and contented himself that everything was right and ready to go. The interview lasted 15 minutes or more and at one point, when Cathal Boylan burst through the door of Room 338, Helena put her hands up like an arresting officer and signalled to him to keep quiet. The Keady man was taken aback and reversed out while I carried on answering Jude's questions. It was only at the conclusion of the interview that I discovered that a live audience (of twelve!) had been viewing the whole episode 'live' all the while.

Jude then enquired if any of our viewers wanted to put a question or two at which point someone sent a text wanting me to predict the outcome of Friday night's big Championship match in Pomeroy. The really important stuff, he said, pointing out that Jude's interview with me wasn't the only Omagh-Carrickmore clash of note this week.

I hear our Niamh is to sing Amhran na bhFiann at the start of the battle…and it will be a battle.

Let me tell you what I am doing as MLA

I have been pursuing a number of crucial health service issues in the past week. This entailed attendance at an MLA / MP Briefing by senior managers of the Western Health

Trust, the tabling of related questions in the Assembly and direct meetings with constituents who have various concerns. I spoke to one of our local papers in general terms about a number of these issues at the start of last week without compromising constituent confidentiality, of course.

I was disappointed when none of this was carried in the paper which subsequently then highlighted a letter from a reader entitled, 'What are our MLAs doing ?' It was clear from the letter to the editor that the reader was focusing on health issues. I can only speak for myself but I know what I am doing. I am lobbying for acute mental health services to be an integral part of the new, enhanced local hospital being built in Omagh.

I am keeping the pressure on the Department of Health to build new primary care centres in Carrickmore and Fintona because the physical accommodation in both places is inadequate.

I am fighting, with others,the proposed closure of Dromore Day Centre. I am highlighting the need for community nurses and carers to receive more support and more resources. I am involved in countless individual issues trying to help people but their right to privacy precludes me from saying too much here.

You would think that those who publicly question what an MLA is doing would at least allow the likes of me to respond.

To not allow this is like saying, 'I want to ask you a question but I do not want to hear your answer.' Sometimes sections of the media complain that 'our politicians' (as if everyone is the same) are not interested in the real issues.

I would hate to think that Danny might be messin' about

Meanwhile on Tuesday, Martin McGuinness was reporting back to the Assembly on the most recent meeting of the North South Ministerial Council which was held in the capital.

I scanned the accompanying written statement for any mention of the A5 Road and put my name down to ask Martin a question.Before I was called to speak, Bronwyn McGahan got her chance and she enquired about the next steps in the process of securing the green light for this crucial road project to re-commence.

Martin's answer was that UUP Minister Danny Kennedy is expected to bring a paper to the Executive in the next couple of weeks with ' Draft Orders' to be issued. Reading between the lines, I formed the impression that Danny could be messing about with something that he should not be messing about with. I tried to put Martin over it again but he said little more than placing the onus on Danny Kennedy to bring forward this paper on schedule.

Wishing a sound Armagh man a full recovery

Some posts on Facebook travel further and reach more people than others. I knew instinctively that a support message for Cathal Boylan would fit this category. Cathal, who has just undergone a major operation, is very popular. Ian Milne and I both serve on the Assembly's Environment Committee with Cathal and we describe him as 'our leader.' Sean McPeake and Conor Keenan have always entered into the spirit of this.

From the Keady area, Cathal is a proud Armagh man. He and his family have a great awareness of the issue of emigration, much of this emanating from personal experience. At Stormont, Cathal really is on top of his game and demonstrates a real understanding of the detail of the legislative process. He talks about 'affirmative resolutions' and how to improve regulations 'on the face of the bill' with a surprising fluency. Sartorially, Cathal is always well turned out and wears the most stylish shirts and ties.

He enjoys the lighter moments for sure when conducting his plenary day visits to all our individual visits on the third floor. Everybody likes to see Cathal arriving on the scene and handshakes are regularly exchanged as if we were meeting for the first time. Cathal comes from a hurling stronghold and likes to take a caman in his hand and show us how to hold it properly. I have known Cathal to celebrate a wee bit too much when his team wins.

We all wish Cathal a speedy and full recovery and send best wishes, too, to Veronica, Cathal's wife. Veronica has acknowledged our support for Cathal in a comment on my Facebook message which I posted on Wednesday evening.

tyronemansblog

July

Our first proper family holiday in 20 years

In all of twenty years, we had never done a proper foreign holiday. This year, I resolved to change this for the good of our family (and the price of a small 2007 car). I booked a week in Catalonia, Barcelona to be precise. The Credit Union, Dublin Airport and Aer Lingus took care of the first bits.

Our holiday apartment was located in Carrer de la Indústria, quite close to Hospital de Pau. The regular sound of emergency ambulancias told us that it was a significant hospital. Wasn't I quare 'n delighted then to learn that we were also within easy walking distance of Basílica de la Sagrada Família. Our visit to this amazing church with its sheer scale as well as its truly unique façades and towers was a definite highlight

This is the great unfinished work of Antoni Gaudi, sometimes referred to as God's Architect (1852 – 1926).

Outside this special place has to be the modern 'selfie'-capital of Europe, such are the numbers of people taking pictures on the wide pavements and in front of the many stalls. We were fiercely impressed and Paula couldn't help herself, succumbing to buy her very own selfie-stick, with Patrick and I slagging her the whole way.

My late Father loved working as a foreman in chapel building works but this would have taken Daddy's imagination to a completely new level. He would have appreciated the craftsmanship far better than me.

Thousands of people are there all of the time, it would appear, and the architecture, still under construction and renewal from its start date in 1882, is unforgettable. The Church is described as 'a Barcelona landmark and an artistic and spiritual symbol of Catalonia.'

Sitting out under a canapé in a side-street lined with trees, in the east of Barcelona on a hot Sunday evening in early July, we ate paella and omelettes. We were also under the shadow of the cranes and towers of this mighty church, not one of my most difficult life experiences to date, I can assure you.

Our Patrick got ready to come on for Lionel himself

I think I can 'get' this Barcelona – 'Més que un club' thing. In truth, most GAA people should understand the Barça phenomenon because their own club will inevitably be more than a club. We know this ourselves Carrickmore. It helps massively, of course, to go to Camp Nou. The nearest thing to Camp Nou has to be Pairc an Chrócaigh.

The sacredness of these two stadia to people the world over, but in Catalonia and Ireland, in particular, is comparable and we should remember that our own headquarters in Dublin is at least equal in terms of historical and national symbolism. We have no call for inferiority complexes on that score. Our taxi driver was a Real Madrid supporter but overcame his prejudices to drop us off anyway on Saturday morning 4 July.

Banners declaring support for FCB and for Catalonian 'independència' were on display from many high-up apartments in the approaching streets.

Pitch-side awakes and fills up your senses more than any other part of the experience. Even the Qatar Airways seats in the dugouts hold you in awe when you stare at them. Patrick and I imagined springing out of them to come on for the injured Messi and Neymar. Patrick never told me this but I know my son well enough. I could see him fix his socks and stand beside the linesman holding up the Number 10 sign, getting ready to high five Lionel himself.

Barcelona (FCB) has become an unbelievable brand. Serious money changes hands in the club's Superstore day in, day out for jerseys, fridge magnets and a whole range of other marketing products. Messi's artistry holds everyone in awe and to watch his childhood promise back in Argentina on Barça TV and in the famous club museum transported my mind to Glencull and Killarney. We have our own Messis in those places.

Different story back home

I was sitting outside Camp Nou for the third time during our week away. I had just bought a new pair of runners at L'Illa Diagonal – 170 shops under the one roof – and I was putting them on in the shade because the heat was muy grande. I walked over to the recycling bins and deposited my old runners which I'd had for too long and which owed me nothing. They were becoming frayed, the sole was thinning and their time was surely up.

People of all nationalities and with varying degrees of coolness and colour walked up and down past me as I drank my water and turned a few pages of the book I had purchased at Dublin Airport; 'Mindfulness' pocketbook by Gill Hasson. Buy one and get the other half price. I swear I saw the girl from the Kellogg's Special K ad on the TV go past wearing a red dress.

I decided to consult my mobile phone which, by design, I had hardly used since our arrival the previous Thursday night. Save to take some holiday photos, that is, and to read The Irish News online. Both Barry McColgan and Helena had been texting and I noticed a few missed calls from media outlets back home, including The Ulster Herald.

On opening up the texts, I learned that an anonymous caller had phoned our office in Omagh to say that a bomb had been left at our house and at our office in Omagh as well. Oh yes, and I was to be shot. Apparently, the Sinn Féin offices in Belfast's Sevastopol Street had received a similar call, naming Jim McVeigh and Gerry Adams as being in their sight lines.

When I looked up, Paula and Patrick came walking out of the stadium, through the doors of FC Botiga. The man himself had a wide beaming smile, a bag under his arm and looked as if he had just signed professional terms with FCB.

Good priests deserve our support in their times of need

I called to see Monsignor Joseph Donnelly at the Parochial House in Omagh early on Saturday evening last. I had just attended the Tyrone versus Meath match at Healy Park on a very wet afternoon where you absolutely needed a coat even if the calendar page told you it was mid-July.

While most cars headed out of the town, I navigated my way to Castle Street and then Brook Street. My visit was prompted by an armed robbery at the Parochial House and another nearby church property earlier that morning.

I simply wanted to convey my own support for the priests in Omagh as well as the solidarity of the wider community, of course.

I respect the many good priests that we have in Tyrone and throughout Ireland. They support us in our times of need and they deserve our support in their times of need.

A quiet man by nature, Monsignor Donnelly is an excellent leader in so many respects.

We shouldn't take men like him for granted and we should adopt a zero tolerance for the type of criminality that was visited upon him and one of his fellow priests last Saturday.

Sometimes families just need extra support

I gained considerable insight this week into the stressful nature of caring for a child with complex needs. I attended a meeting with senior health professionals and a couple regarding plans to reduce the level of care being provided for a little child, the couple's child who has had serious health problems since birth.

I don't want to sound patronising but the parents are doing their absolute best to deal with health risk situations every day and they administer medication around the clock.

Their efforts are truly heroic and, without going into all the details, I have formed the opinion that they need more help than that which is being offered by the Health Trust at this time. The health professionals who ultimately determine the level of care and support did listen and engaged sympathetically. But there are 'criteria' for this and 'criteria' for that. Inevitably, there are budgetary restrictions. Both parents are stretched to the limit trying to manage direct payments, trying to secure a night's sleep, having to become medical experts, trying to live and not merely exist, watching their child make progress slowly and incrementally, asking for help.

This case is on-going and I will remain involved offering support to the parents, as best I can, by way of giving them time when they contact me and by challenging the Trust to provide a proper care package which will meet the holistic needs of the child and family.

I reckon that thousands of families are in situations like this, the length and breadth of Ireland.

Uncle Joe rang to tell me some big family news

My Uncle Joe phoned during the week to break some 'big family news' to me. Joe always speaks some Gaelic in his conversations as he is a strong Gaeilgeoir. Although reared himself in Loughmacrory, Joe has lived in Dublin for many years and at one point in his life, he ran a very successful paint and decoration business in Bray. Joe and Finola have always been proud of their only son, Brian and of their three daughters, Anne, Eimear and Orla.

Career-wise, they have all done very well but I will take a risk now and say that Brian has perhaps distinguished himself most in this respect. In the past week, Brian was appointed Irish Ambassador to India, Nepal and Sri Lanka. Previously, Brian was the Ambassador to Slovakia and he held other senior roles in Moscow and Stockholm before that.

The Department of Foreign Affairs has been good to Brian and he has been good to it (DFA). We are all made different and some would not share this news publicly. But I am also proud of Brian's achievements and as Joe said to me on the phone, 'forgive me for a wee bit of bragging on this occasion.' Guím rath agus blath ar Bhrian sna laethanta atá roimhe. Tá bród orainn as.

Joe's next phone call was to his niece, my cousin, Ann Marie (Fitzgerald, Councillor) to tell her his latest scéal. I told Joe that I would tell Kevin and the others as he was on holiday. We all hope to meet up soon to say Slán leis.

If you want to reach my friend, leave him alone

Like everyone else, I have more 'friends' in the Facebook sense than I do in the real sense. You know what I mean even if technically, I have a like page on Fb and not a friend page as such. One of my real friends has told me that to a certain degree at least, he has opted for solitude in his life. He loves good quotes, he says, because they are the distilled wisdom of the ages.

He tells me that 'solitude can be a sanctuary or a prison, a heaven or a hell, as we ourselves make it.' He reminds us that 'Lord Byron' only ever went out ' to get me a fresh appetite for being alone.' He tells me that 'not all who wander are lost' and that people, according to Socrates, should 'beware the barrenness of a busy life.'

One of his favourites is a quote from Sheryl Crow; '…if you like to reach me leave me alone…' This man writes a lot of poetry and he believes, as Aristotle did, that 'poetry is finer and more philosophical than history' because 'poetry expresses the universal, and history only the particular.' I drive past this man's house quite often on the road to Dublin.

I know he is at home and sometimes I stop off with him to exchange our wisdoms. The last day I called, he told me that Maslow reckoned that 'A musician must make music, an artist must paint, a poet must write if he is to be ultimately at peace with himself. What one can be, one must be.'

tyronemansblog

August

Bláthnaid had a top-up in her phone

Our Bláthnaid went to Dublin on Wednesday. I dropped her off at Omagh Bus Station at 10am and picked her up again after one in the morning. She had a top-up in her phone and not a care in the world, I'd say, as I watched her walk to the summer seat in front of the depot. She was heading to yet another concert. But of course 'all my friends go to far more concerts than I do.'

I don't remember the name of the group from California which 'headlined' at The Academy in Abbey Street, within walking distance, of Busáras but I do know that 'Amoré' or some similar version of that word features in the second half of the band's title.

We kept in touch by text throughout the day. She got to meet the band and seemed positively pleased with herself when

the drummer, Elliott thanked her for travelling to the concert
from Tyrone as they hadn't been able to make it up North
on this occasion.

Bláthnaid usually comes home from concerts with the date
for the next one imprinted on her mind. At any given time,
she might have eight or nine mapped out. 'Surely not on a
week evening during school-term, Bláthnaid.'

Meanwhile, I sit outside bus stations waiting for her return
and to assist her on the last leg of that particular (long) day's
travelling. 'Excuse me, What time is the Bus Éireann due
in, le do thoil ?'

**I think the comrades I left behind
will have understood**

As in any political party (or Movement), within Sinn Féin
there is a certain amount of discipline and a certain amount
of flexibility or even scope for individuality. Some internal
meetings are MANDATORY for elected representatives
within the party, however, and you would need a very good
reason not to be there.

Last Saturday morning, Sinn Féin at Cúige level held a very
important internal seminar in The Strule Arts Centre in
Omagh.

They came from all areas across the North and the lecture theatre or Minor Hall was full to capacity. I had the duty of chairing the meeting not least because we were hosting the meeting in Omagh. I had a wee dilemma in that I needed to be away before the end of the event. To be straight about it, I could hear the clarion call of Croke Park and the Tyrone versus Monaghan All Ireland Quarter Final.

In truth, I needed to be at Tamnamore Roundabout for a quarter past twelve. The throw-in was at four o'clock.
My remit was to introduce the proceedings and key speakers and to invite questions and comments from the floor. So Far, So Good…so to speak:

I fulfilled this role precisely, facilitating debate and keeping order. It was a case of so far, so good for the first ninety minutes, I felt, but then my time came and it took all my experience and whatever political guile I may or may not possess to vacate the chair half-way through the seminar and manoeuvre Michaela Boyle into the chair. This was during one of the key presentations to party members when everyone was paying attention to Sean Mag Uidhir. I needed to disappear without any fuss or attention. I had the car parked in such a manner as to affect a quick escape.

Michaela co-operated fully when I sent her down a wee note and she became my 'impact sub', going on to preside over the rest of the meeting seamlessly and with great professionalism. At least I was told this much in a text message from Barry McColgan two hours later. I duly read his text after handing over my €1.90 at the Toll Plaza near Drogheda. I think the comrades I left behind will have understood my premature exit. The traffic was serious on the M1 to Dublin.

Oisin is disturbed that he is now a museum piece

'Is that where they have me now?' Oisin McConville said to me on Monday when I told him that I had seen a great picture of him in the Croke Park Museum the day before. I like Oisin McConville. I think legendary forwards appreciate each other.

Seriously, the museum in Croke Park is a great experience. They have the sense, too, to show Mugsy's goal against Dublin over and over again on a big screen because that goal was as much a piece of art as a Yeats poem.

I saw Peter the Great on the wall, too, and Mark Donnelly as well. Tommy Traynor of Errigal Ciaran told me that he wished he had taken a photo of me, a Carrickmore man, taking a picture of Peter, an Errigal Ciaran man. Just like Kilmainham Gaol and The GPO, put the Croke Park Museum down on your itinerary the next time you visit the capital. I heard during the week that Jimmy Barry Murphy and Jimmy Keaveney were inducted into the Hall of Greats. Nothing wrong with those decisions.

tyronemansblog

September

Sean wasn't phased by the best of them

© Jason Moncrieff Photography

Corner-backs have come and gone. One of the most uncompromising – and this is putting it mildly – of them all was Sean Donnelly who played for Trillick and Tyrone.

I attract laughs and funny stares from people who know him when I tell them that 'I am not afraid of Sean Donnelly.' It sounds good to me when I say it.

The photo above shows the two of us at Trillick's Strictly Red. Sean's son Seanie was one of the dancers.

Throughout the evening, We listed and named forwards who had the privilege of being marked by Sean (literally).

Sean wasn't overawed by the best of them and that illustrious list included Mickey Linden.

Iggy Gallagher accused me of 'licking up' to Sean Donnelly on the evening and wondered where all my tough talk had gone.

Everybody only has small number of real friends

I have seven or eight friends with whom I have a strong connection. Sometimes, however, I become so caught up with what I am doing on a day to day, week to week basis that I let things drift and I let months go by without my being in contact with them.

Sometimes I write their initials on the margins of my week plan and stare at them to see if I can be a better friend myself. Who was it that said that to get a friend, you have to be one?

On Saturday past, I 'made the effort' and I ring-fenced half a day to reconnect with a man who lives in a different town than me, a different county than me, in fact a different province.

Firstly, I ascertained that he and his wife were going to be at Home. Then, I headed off and was delayed a bit because of a Last Saturday feeder parade in Clogher.

It took me two hours to reach my friend's house, an impressive bungalow in the country.

When I arrived, I parked up and let myself in the back door. It was good to meet up again because people tend only to have a small number of friends in whose company they feel comfortable and in whom they trust. Leaving it too long to say 'Hello' can be a bad thing, however, because after a few minutes of light-hearted conversation, my friend said to me: 'Did you hear about my Mother ?'
I knew by his tone that he was creating space for something that was serious and necessary.
'My Mother died and her funeral was last week.'
When I was leaving a couple of ours later, I resolved to my friend and to myself to make a better effort to keep in touch with those I consider to be my real friends.

I got the loan of Mickey Treanor's dickey bow

I was delighted to receive an invitation to their 2015 Ulster GAA All-Stars Dinner in Armagh City Hotel last Thursday night. The Dinner is a highlight for me every year and I was able to bring Patrick along with me as my guest.

But then we faced quite a challenge as we needed two dickey bows. I searched every drawer in our house but I could only turn up one. This meant that I had no dickey bow as we departed Carrickmore for the black tie dinner in Armagh.

I thought I would try my neighbour, Minty but he wasn't there and Sheena could only locate a couple of cartoon-y ones belonging to wee Caodhan. They wouldn't do. As we passed Treanor's, I knew Mickey was nearly bound to be a tux – type of a man and fair play to Aisling, Alannah and Michaela, they pinpointed for me what I needed.

Two top men in our dickey bows straightened our collars going through Pomeroy, then..me and our Patrick.
We had a great evening at Noel Doran's (Editor) Table; Table4, and so, too, was the guest speaker, Mícheál Ó Muircheartaigh and Michelle and Jimmy. Patrick reckons that he wasn't at all bored listening to Mícheál as 'he knows an awful lot of stuff.' Mícheál was a tour de force as usual both Gaeilge and in English; telling stories.

Patrick got photographs taken with Mícheál and with the best forwards in Ulster, Conor McManus and Michael Murphy among them. Three Tyrone players were selected this year: Mattie Donnelly, Peter Harte and Sean Cavanagh. Lynette Fay did her best on stage to persuade each of them to articulate their pride but those men typically do their talking on the pitch.

Whether Mickey Treanor ever knew I had borrowed his dickey bow or not, I am not sure. What I do know is that when I left it back the next evening, Mickey's daughters couldn't understand why anyone would leave it so late to get ready for a black tie dinner.

I like Jimmy Durante's advice

One of the CDs that I have listened to quite a bit recently in the car is one where Barry Manilow sings duets with legendary artists who are deceased. This is an upbeat CD and one that is best listened to with the volume turned up high.

I know that this type of 'Duets with the Legends' CD sounds rare but I'll try to explain. Manilow went into a studio and, taking advantage of technology, and creating an audio marvel, sang in concert with recordings of Whitney Houston, John Denver, Judy Garland, Louis Armstrong, Marilyn Monroe and other stars who are no longer with us.

At the start, he 'teams up' and 'dialogues' with Jimmy Durante (1893 – 1980) to whom he turns for advice on the challenge of singing with the legends, an undertaking which he finds a bit overwhelming. Durante was a singer, pianist and comedian from New York who knew his stuff. 'What chance do I have, Mr. Durante?' asked Barry and Mr. Durante replied, 'All the chance in the world!'

Durante's advice was for him / us all to 'sing from the heart' and he further explains that 'heart' is what gave Bing Crosby the edge on stage more than his voice. I like this sentiment because whatever you do in life, it is very important that you sing from the heart.

I told this to a large number of Sinn Féin activists near Drogheda last Friday and Martin McGuinness told us that he once met Bing Crosby's nephew. When Gerry Adams started to croon like Bing, Mary Lou jokingly wondered aloud if Section 31 and censorship in its day didn't have some upsides.

Goalkeepers are a rare breed for sure

I am sure Niall Morgan won't mind my sharing with the whole world a snippet from a conversation we had while sitting in the Nally Stand during the recent Dromore / Omagh Championship Quarter Final in Carrickmore.

We were talking about professional goalkeepers who ply their trade in England. Niall casually remarked that a man called Richard Wright is the third goalkeeper for Manchester

City, I think he said, and he earns £30,000 a week 'for sitting in the stand.'

Niall didn't say it but I think he was inferring that he could do with a slice of that action. Nice work if you could get it. Niall's girlfriend was sitting beside him and she gestured with her eyes that that would suit her down to the ground.

Down in front of us, Ryan Clarke and Peter Ward were the last line of defence for their clubs. I salute all goalkeepers from Big Oz to Niall Morgan for they are a rare breed indeed.

Soldiers staring across at each other

The Unionist parties at Stormont love their former British soldiers. Several occupy the blue benches of the Assembly Chamber.

Last week, Mike Nesbitt probably thought that he pulled a flanker on Peter Robinson when he appointed the UUP Andy Allen to their MLA team as a co-option in place of their now former East Belfast MLA, Michael Copeland. Reportedly, he did this without consulting the local party association.

Both Copeland (UDR, I think) and Allen pulled on the British uniform and both are living with the legacy of war with injuries, both physical and mental. Allen suffered horrendous injuries in Afghanistan, far from his home.

There are others in the Assembly Chamber, people who are elected with strong mandates, who were soldiers on the other side. These men and women were Volunteer soldiers in the IRA. Alex Kane wrote an article about the new MLA, Andy Allen in last Saturday's 'Belfast Telegraph.'

It was interesting.

tyronemansblog

October

Mammy knew why I was taking so long to close the front door

An issue that is brought up with me time and time again is the desire of a family member to succeed the tenancy of a Housing Executive house which has become vacant as a result of the death of a parent. Or perhaps one of the parents has to go into a Home for specialist care.

Without going into all the details, and respecting the need for the Housing Executive to allocate houses on the basis of objective need, what this really points up for me is the emotional attachment of many to 'the home house'. I know the feeling.

For a year or so after Mammy and Daddy died, it was an empty feeling to drive past Termon Crescent and to have no call or reason to stop off. Thankfully, a member of my family does now live in our 'home house' and things are much better as a consequence of this.

When my Mother was alive but had declining eyesight, she used to count how long it took me to get from the sitting room to the front door when I was leaving. If it took a little longer than it should have, Mammy knew that I was 'stealing' a tin of diet coke, a wee orange or a banana from the cloakroom. She would often accuse me.

It helped when Fassbender said it

We know it ourselves but it is always good to hear it from an external source. I was delighted, and I am sure you were, too, to hear the distinguished actor, Michael Fassbender speak of his 'respect' for Bobby Sands.

Let us remind ourselves of what Fassbender said when he was interviewed on the BBC's Andrew Marr Show:
'Well I think you know anybody who has the commitment and courage to follow something like that through to hunger strike, you think that the person is extraordinary. He was a leader – that's very clear…having had a minor insight into what it must have been like, I very much have respect for him.'

My uncle Jack was very close to Michael Gaughan who died on hunger strike in England among others, not least Frank

Stagg. I always remember that Sean McCaughey and Martin Hurson came from my own native county. Five of the ten hunger strikers who died in 1981 were from Derry (City and County) and then there was McCreesh, McDonnell and Doherty.

Irish history is littered with many other examples of Republican courage and selflessness. Men from Cork and Galway and other counties also died on hunger strike. We should be very proud to speak their names in any company, at any time.

Impasse needs to be broken in Carrickmore

I tabled a special Adjournment debate in Stormont on Tuesday. An Adjournment debate is always about a subject of local, constituency importance. My chosen topic was 'Spatial Planning to meet housing demand in Carrickmore.' Very local in its relevance.

I briefed the Tyrone Herald about what I was trying to achieve before the debate because, in politics, you need to share with the people what it is you are doing.

Anyway, I spoke for fifteen minutes on my chosen topic and in an attempt to influence the Environment Minister and his senior planning officials who were present in the chamber. Four of the other five MLAs for West Tyrone added their words of support for my initiative, the exception in this case being Tom Buchanan.

The DUP MLA from Drumquin must have figured out that there aren't many votes for him in Carrickmore.

Anyway, my main point was that new land needs to be zoned in the Carrickmore area so that local people can live there. We discussed the ins and outs of it all and how 'nothing has been moving' for years in Carrickmore in respect of housing for a variety of reasons and a combination of circumstances.

It is all recorded in Hansard for the record.

At the conclusion of the debate, I sat down with Minister Mark H Durkan and discussed some additional detail around planning hurdles which need to be removed to 'allow the people to live.'

This is a major priority for me in my local MLA role and I will continue to pursue this agenda.

Those ten boyhood years allow Tyrone to 'claim' Brian Friel

Anna Lo had the presence of mind to request that the Assembly should formally discuss the death of playwright, Brian Friel. This section of the agenda or Order Paper on Monday morning was called a 'Matter of the Day.'

Anna paid her tribute and so did Martin McGuinness. Martin had attended Brian's funeral in Donegal the previous day. Martin always seems to be in the right place at the right time. Others who rose to pay tribute included Colm Eastwood, Leslie Cree and David McNarry.

I indicated myself that I wanted to say a few words and to express 'mo chomhbhrón lena mhuintir'. I wanted to claim one of Ireland's finest as 'a Tyrone man.' Yes, he left Killyclogher with his family to take up residence in Derry when he was ten years of age but those ten years are crucial and allow us to claim him.

Of course, Derry and Donegal have strong claims over Brian's identity but we in Tyrone need to contest this territory. We don't concede our artists too handy. In my remarks, I also mentioned two other great writers who came from the Omagh district... Alice Milligan and Benedict Kiely.

I gave the Mid Ulster Drama Festival an honourable mention in the chamber, pointing out that a Friel play was always a high point for those of us reared on 'Nine Nights of Theatre' in The Patrician Hall. I also said that the local government authorities in Donegal, Derry and Omagh will want to, in time, acknowledge the legacy of Brian Friel in a thought out and appropriate manner.

'Definition of happiness...
a size 5 O'Neill's between hand and toe.'